19th August 2012

I

helpful in your prayer-
life. May God continue
to bless you richly.

Love,
Clay

The Daily Prayer Rosary

Rosary Meditations through the day and through the Christian year using resources from Common Worship

Compiled by

Clay Roundtree

CANTERBURY
PRESS
Norwich

© J.C Roundtree 2011, in this compilation

Common Worship is copyright © The Archbishops' Council,
2000–2006. Material from this work is reproduced with permission.

Published in 2011 by Canterbury Press

Editorial office
13–17 Long Lane,
London EC1A 9PN, UK

Canterbury Press is an imprint of Hymns Ancient and Modern Ltd
(a registered charity)
13a Hellesdon Park Road, Norwich, Norfolk, NR6 5DR

www.scm-canterburypress.co.uk

British Library Cataloguing in Publication data

A catalogue record for this book is available
from the British Library

978 1-84825-088-8

Typeset by *Church Times*

Printed and bound by
T. J. International, Padstow, Cornwall

Contents

For Crispin, Jude and Isaac

Acknowledgements

I would like to thank the Archbishops' Council for permission to use materials from *Common Worship* for this publication, and I give my sincere thanks to Alexandra Bellamy for providing a drawing for the rosary diagram. I am grateful to the parishioners of St Francis of Assisi Ingleby Barwick, the students of All Saints CE VA Secondary School Ingleby Barwick and the ordinands of Westcott House, Cambridge who have prayed these and other rosary meditations, which has helped me form their structure and purpose. Finally, my thanks to the Revd Paul Dominiak for his encouragement in developing this idea and especially to my wife Frances for her love and support.

Introduction

This book combines two elements familiar to many Christians but not usually thought of together: prayer with rosary beads and the songs and psalms of the Bible. Prayer beads are used all over the world by millions and come in a staggering variety of forms; even in the Roman Catholic Church there are a number of alternatives to the most widely recognizable form of prayer beads, the rosary. The various meditations here are made up of the psalms and biblical canticles as they are found in the Church of England's library of resources known as *Common Worship*. These biblical texts provide the structure of four Offices: Morning Prayer, Prayer through the Day, Evening Prayer and Night Prayer, as well as eight meditations for use through the Church's year. In combining the rosary of the Church and the songs of the Bible, one is presented with a devotional approach to praying scripture in a tactile way.

The traditional way of praying the rosary already engages with scripture in a series of meditations on the events of Christ's life, known as mysteries. This is a very rich and wonderful way to enter the great story of salvation that we know in Christ Jesus.[1] However, in my experience as an Anglican priest, I have found that many Anglicans simply do not feel comfortable with the thought of praying the rosary or have had no experience of it. These Christians have been in mind when compiling these meditations, and it is my

---

1 The method presented here is not meant to replace or belittle the traditional approach, but simply to introduce the rosary to people who had not previously given it any serious thought. Many Church of England people have never prayed with a rosary before, and perhaps it is equally true that many of the canticles and prayers found in *Common Worship* are not as well known as they should or could be.

hope that they may in time come to feel quite relaxed with the thought of praying with a set of rosary beads in hand. Some Christians in the Methodist tradition will know that John Wesley himself prayed with a rosary from time to time.[2]

Obviously, one does not need a set of beads in order to pray. In fact, all that is required to pray is a willing attentiveness to God. But there are millions of Christians who have found beads to be a comforting prayer tool. Beads offer a way of externalizing our prayers, reminding us that prayer is not something that simply goes on inside our heads. As part of the Body of Christ, we are accustomed to worshipping God with our bodies through postures of prayer, the sacraments, and actions such as sharing the Peace. Prayer is a physical reality, and prayer beads of any sort reinforce that fact.

Some accounts of the origin of the rosary suggest that beads were originally given to those who wished to participate in the monastic rhythm of prayer through the day. They were given a form of prayer that was repetitive, contemplative, and elegant: the Hail Mary. Most Christians in the West are literate today, and are very capable of reading the monastic Daily Office if they wish to do so, at least in translation. The rosary then can have a different purpose for literate Christians, serving as an aide for focusing on the words of scripture, and then ultimately to move the individual beyond the words to a relationship with almighty God and communion with him.

The rosary is instantly recognizable in popular culture and with young people, even if they don't know exactly what it is for. When I have led prayers with teenagers using the rosary, most have been captivated by it. I have found that young people soon become bored or distracted with printed liturgies. This is not a criticism of the texts, but a comment on the attention span of some of the young people I have prayed with. This changed dramatically when we began praying with the rosary in hand. Prayer became much more concentrated, giving them literally something to hold on to. This has enabled me to find another way of practising the presence of God with them, not just merely talking about him. It also presents a way

---

2 J. Neville Ward *The Use of Praying* Epworth, 1977.

of bringing together the different kinds of prayer: praise, adoration, penitence, oblation and intercessory prayer.

Our minds often wander in flights of fancy when we pray and many have found it helps to have something solid to hold on to, using our sense of touch: just consider the popularity of the holding cross. Christian prayer is always offered through Christ who is our rock, and the beads of the rosary serve as little weights to keep us anchored to the rock. The physicality of the beads is important in the same way that the sacraments are: Christ gave us sacraments to minister to the whole person: body and soul. The rosary has a sacramental quality, keeping prayer rooted in our bodies, just as other outward signs, like bread, wine, oil and water, point us to an inward spiritual reality.

Prayer with a rosary can feel a bit like going on a journey, a journey that begins and ends with the cross. The cross on the end of the rosary reminds us we are not climbing a spiritual ladder when we pray but returning to the foot of the cross, the place where the love of God shone most brightly for humanity. We also consider the words of Jesus when he tells his disciples to 'take up your cross and follow me' (Mark 8.34). In our Christian journey we always need to return to the basics, and each time we do, we find new insights and greater spiritual depth. The rosary meditations here help us return to the basics by reading God's word as prayer. St Dominic, as the legend goes, gave the rosary to the illiterate so they could count the psalms as they heard them sung by literate monks and nuns. In our own day, we are privileged to have immediate access to scripture. The rosary meditations here in this book can help us learn to pray through the words of scripture in an unhurried and contemplative way.

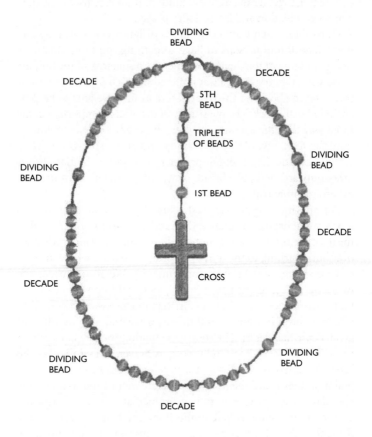

DIVIDING BEAD

DECADE

DECADE

5TH BEAD

TRIPLET OF BEADS

DIVIDING BEAD

DIVIDING BEAD

1ST BEAD

DECADE

DECADE

CROSS

DECADE

DIVIDING BEAD

DIVIDING BEAD

DECADE

Praying the Meditations

Begin by holding the cross on the stem of the rosary and say the opening prayers. Move to the first bead and say the opening verse. There are three beads grouped together on the stem referred to here as the 'triplet of beads', and they are numbered 2, 3 and 4. There is one last bead on the stem known here as the 'fifth bead'. The 'dividing beads' are there to set apart the five decades of the rosary. Simply move slowly from dividing bead to the first decade and make your way around the loop of beads. Each of the five sections of ten beads (decades) of the rosary takes a psalm or canticle, a litany or intercessory prayers and divides them into verses: *one verse per bead*. These can be adapted for personal use, and favourite prayers and verses of scripture can easily be inserted on the dividing beads. A particular prayer intention may be announced before each decade, i.e., 'in this decade we pray for (e.g. the mission of the Church, the leaders of the world, the sick, etc.) …' The *Cycle of Intercession* has been adapted from *Common Worship Daily Prayer* to be used with each decade, or, other more personal intentions can be made. Take your time as you say the words of the canticles and take a breath at the asterisk, halfway through each verse. Do not be tempted to ignore the pause at the mid-point of the verse: the silence allows the words to resonate. Having a pause at the mid-point of the verse is an ancient tradition, giving the opportunity to reflect on what is being said as well as being a practical way of learning to listen carefully to the other voices with whom you are praying. If the meditation is said with others, choose someone to lead with the rest of the group responding with the words in **bold type**. It may take practice, but continue to observe the asterisk at the mid-point of the verse even in a group setting. The meditation will of course need practising, so try not to get frustrated if you lose your place on the rosary. Any new prayer method we discover takes practice and perseverance for it to bear fruit.

Finally, Christian prayer is ultimately about being caught up in the life of the Trinity, and perhaps this is represented in some way by the circle of beads itself. The circle may also remind us that when we pray in faith we are not alone but joined with the Church, the choirs of angels, the saints today and of old, and blessed Mary, who brought forth into the world the Word, stood under the cross at his death, and rejoiced at the resurrection.

The Lord's Prayer and the Apostles' Creed

The Lord's Prayer

Our Father in heaven,
hallowed be your name,
your kingdom come,
your will be done,
on earth as in heaven.
Give us today our daily bread.
Forgive us our sins
as we forgive those who sin
   against us.
Lead us not into temptation
but deliver us from evil.
For the kingdom, the power,
and the glory are yours
now and for ever.
Amen.

Our Father, who art in heaven,
hallowed be thy name;
thy kingdom come;
thy will be done;
on earth as it is in heaven.
Give us this day our daily bread.
And forgive us our trespasses,
as we forgive those who trespass
   against us.
And lead us not into temptation;
but deliver us from evil.
For thine is the kingdom,
the power and the glory,
for ever and ever.
Amen.

The Apostles' Creed

I believe in God, the Father almighty,
creator of heaven and earth.

I believe in Jesus Christ, his only Son, our Lord,
who was conceived by the Holy Spirit,
born of the Virgin Mary,
suffered under Pontius Pilate,

was crucified, died, and was buried;
he descended to the dead.
On the third day he rose again;
he ascended into heaven,
he is seated at the right hand of the Father,
and he will come to judge the living and the dead.

I believe in the Holy Spirit,
the holy catholic Church,
the communion of saints,
the forgiveness of sins,
the resurrection of the body,
and the life everlasting.
Amen.

Cycle of Intercessions

In Ordinary Time

Every day
CROSS: In the morning: the day and its tasks; the world and its needs; the Church and her life
CROSS: In the evening: peace; individuals and their needs

Sunday
1ST DECADE: The universal Church
2ND DECADE: Bishops, synods and all who lead the Church
3RD DECADE: The leaders of the nations
4TH DECADE: The natural world and the resources of the earth
5TH DECADE: All who are in any kind of need

Monday
1ST DECADE: The media and the arts
2ND DECADE: Farming and fishing
3RD DECADE: Commerce and industry
4TH DECADE: Those whose work is unfulfilling, stressful or fraught with danger
5TH DECADE: All who are unemployed

Tuesday
1ST DECADE: All who are sick in body, mind or spirit
2ND DECADE: Those in the midst of famine or disaster
3RD DECADE: Victims of abuse and violence, intolerance and prejudice
4TH DECADE: Those who are bereaved
5TH DECADE: All who work in the medical and healing professions

9

Wednesday
1ST DECADE: The social services
2ND DECADE: All who work in the criminal justice system
3RD DECADE: Victims and perpetrators of crime
4TH DECADE: The work of aid agencies throughout the world
5TH DECADE: Those living in poverty or under oppression

Thursday
1ST DECADE: Local government, community leaders
2ND DECADE: All who provide local services
3RD DECADE: Those who work with young or elderly people
4TH DECADE: Schools, colleges and universities
5TH DECADE: Emergency and rescue organizations

Friday
1ST DECADE: The Queen, members of parliament and the
    armed forces
2ND DECADE: Peace and justice in the world
3RD DECADE: Those who work for reconciliation
4TH DECADE: All whose lives are devastated by war and civil strife
5TH DECADE: Prisoners, refugees and homeless people

Saturday
1ST DECADE: Our homes, families, friends and all whom we love
2ND DECADE: Those whose time is spent caring for others
3RD DECADE: Those who are close to death
4TH DECADE: Those who have lost hope
5TH DECADE: The worship of the Church

In Seasonal Time

Every day
CROSS: In the morning: the day and its tasks; the world and its
    needs; the Church and her life
CROSS: In the evening: peace; individuals and their needs

Advent

1ST DECADE: The Church, that she may be ready for the coming of Christ

2ND DECADE: The leaders of the Church

3RD DECADE: The nations, that they may be subject to the rule of God

4TH DECADE: Those who are working for justice in the world

5TH DECADE: The broken, that they may find God's healing

Christmas

1ST DECADE: The Church, especially in places of conflict

2ND DECADE: The Holy Land, for peace with justice, and reconciliation

3RD DECADE: Refugees and asylum seekers

4TH DECADE: Homeless people

5TH DECADE: Families with young children

Epiphany

1ST DECADE: The unity of the Church

2ND DECADE: The peace of the world

3RD DECADE: The healing of the sick

4TH DECADE: The revelation of Christ to those from whom his glory is hidden

5TH DECADE: All who travel

Lent

1ST DECADE: Those preparing for baptism and confirmation

2ND DECADE: Those serving through leadership

3RD DECADE: Those looking for forgiveness

4TH DECADE: Those misled by the false gods of this present age

5TH DECADE: All who are hungry

Passiontide

1ST DECADE: The persecuted Church

2ND DECADE: The oppressed peoples of the world

3RD DECADE: All who are lonely

4TH DECADE: All who are near to death

5TH DECADE: All who are facing loss

Easter

1ST DECADE: The people of God, that they may proclaim the risen Lord

2ND DECADE: God's creation, that the peoples of the earth may meet their responsibility to care

3RD DECADE: Those in despair and darkness, that they may find the hope and light of Christ

4TH DECADE: Those in fear of death, that they may find faith through the resurrection

5TH DECADE: Prisoners and captives

Pentecost and the Holy Spirit

1ST DECADE: God's royal priesthood, for empowerment by the Spirit

2ND DECADE: Those who wait on God, that they may find renewal

3RD DECADE: All people, that they may acknowledge the kingdom of the ascended Christ

4TH DECADE: The earth, for productivity and for fruitful harvests

5TH DECADE: All who are struggling with broken relationships

All Saints to Advent

1ST DECADE: The saints on earth, that they may live as citizens of heaven

2ND DECADE: All people, that they may hear and believe the word of God

3RD DECADE: All who fear the winter months

4TH DECADE: All sovereigns and political leaders, that they may imitate the righteous rule of Christ

5TH DECADE: All who grieve or wait with the dying

Part One: Daily Prayer with the Rosary

Morning Prayer

CROSS

In the name of the Father and of the Son and of the Holy Spirit.
Amen.

The Lord's Prayer

As our Saviour taught us, so we pray
Our Father in heaven …

(or)

Let us pray with confidence as our Saviour has taught us
Our Father, who art in heaven …

The Apostles' Creed

I believe in God …

1ST BEAD

O Lord, open our lips.
And our mouth shall proclaim your praise.

Glory to the Father and to the Son
and to the Holy Spirit;
as it was in the beginning is now
and shall be for ever. Amen.

TRIPLET OF BEADS

2 Seek the Lord while he may be found,
call upon him while he is near.

3 Let the wicked abandon their ways
and the unrighteous their thoughts.

4 Turn back to the Lord, who will have mercy;
to our God who will richly pardon.

cf Isaiah 55

5TH BEAD

Blessed are you, Lord our God,
creator and redeemer of all;
to you be glory and praise for ever.
From the waters of chaos you drew forth the world
and in your great love fashioned us in your image.
Now, through the deep waters of death,
you have brought your people to new birth
by raising your Son to life in triumph.
May Christ your light ever dawn in our hearts
as we offer you our sacrifice of thanks and praise.
Blessed be God, Father, Son and Holy Spirit.
Blessed be God for ever.

DIVIDING BEAD

Let the words of my mouth and the meditation of my heart
**be acceptable in your sight, O Lord,
my strength and my redeemer.**

Psalm 19.14

Silence is kept.

*Before each decade begins, a prayer intention may be announced.
The cycle of intercession on pages 9–10 may be used.*

1ST DECADE   *A Song of Triumph*

1 May Christ the daystar dawn in our hearts *
   and triumph over the shades of night.

2 **O come, let us sing to the Lord; ***
   let us heartily rejoice in the rock of our salvation.

3 Let us come into his presence with thanksgiving *
   and be glad in him with psalms.

4 **For the Lord is a great God ***
   and a great king above all gods.

5 In his hand are the depths of the earth *
   and the heights of the mountains are his also.

6 **The sea is his, for he made it, ***
   and his hands have moulded the dry land.

7 Come, let us worship and bow down *
   and kneel before the Lord our Maker.

8 **For he is our God; we are the people of his pasture and the**
   sheep of his hand. *
   O that today you would listen to his voice.

from Psalm 95

9 Glory to the Father and to the Son and to the Holy Spirit; *
   As it was in the beginning is now and shall be for ever. Amen.

10 **May Christ the daystar dawn in our hearts ***
   and triumph over the shades of night.

(vs. 1, 10 CW Refrain)

DIVIDING BEAD

My heart tells of your word, 'Seek my face.'
Your face, Lord, will I seek.

Psalm 27.10

Silence is kept.

2ND DECADE   *A song of God's Praise*

1 O God, you are my God; eagerly I seek you; *
   my soul is athirst for you.

2 **My flesh also faints for you, ***
   as in a dry and thirsty land where there is no water.

3 So would I gaze upon you in your holy place, *
    that I might behold your power and your glory.

4 **Your loving-kindness is better than life itself ***
   and so my lips shall praise you.

5 I will bless you as long as I live *
   and lift up my hands in your name.

6 **My soul shall be satisfied, as with marrow and fatness, ***
   and my mouth shall praise you with joyful lips,

7 When I remember you upon my bed *
   and meditate on you in the watches of the night.

8 **For you have been my helper ***
   and under the shadow of your wings will I rejoice.

9 My soul clings to you; *
   your right hand shall hold me fast.

Psalm 63.1-9

10 **Glory to the Father and to the Son and to the Holy Spirit;** *
   as it was in the beginning is now and shall be for ever. Amen.

DIVIDING BEAD

To you, O Lord, I lift up my soul.
O my God, in you I trust.

Psalm 25.1a

Silence is kept.

3ᴿᴰ DECADE   *A Song of Redemption*

1 Christ is the image of the invisible God, *
   the firstborn of all creation.

2 **The Father has delivered us from the dominion of darkness,** *
   and transferred us to the kingdom of his beloved Son;

3 In whom we have redemption, *
   the forgiveness of our sins.

4 **He is the image of the invisible God,** *
   the firstborn of all creation.

5 For in him all things were created, *
   in heaven and on earth, visible and invisible.

6 **All things were created through him and for him,** *
   he is before all things and in him all things hold together.

7 He is the head of the body, the Church, *
   he is the beginning, the firstborn from the dead.

8 **In him all the fullness of God was pleased to dwell;** *
   and through him God was pleased to reconcile all things.

Colossians 1.13-18a,19,20a

9 Glory to the Father and to the Son and to the Holy Spirit; *
 as it was in the beginning is now and shall be for ever. Amen.

10 **Christ is the image of the invisible God, ***
 the firstborn of all creation.

(vs. 1, 10 CW Refrain)

DIVIDING BEAD

Make me to know your ways, O Lord,
and teach me your paths.

Psalm 25.3

Silence is kept.

4ᵀᴴ DECADE *The Song of Zechariah*

1 Blessed be the Lord, the God of Israel, *
 who has come to his people and set them free.

2 **He has raised up for us a mighty Saviour, ***
 born of the house of his servant David.

3 Through his holy prophets, God promised of old *
 to save us from our enemies,
  from the hands of all that hate us.

4 **To show mercy to our ancestors, ***
 and to remember his holy covenant.

5 This was the oath God swore to our father Abraham: *
 to set us free from the hands of our enemies,

6 **Free to worship him without fear, ***
 holy and righteous in his sight all the days of our life.

7 And you, child, shall be called the prophet of the Most High, *
 for you will go before the Lord to prepare his way,

8 **To give his people knowledge of salvation** *
by the forgiveness of all their sins.

9 In the tender compassion of our God *
the dawn from on high shall break upon us,

10 **To shine on those who dwell in darkness**
and the shadow of death, *
and to guide our feet into the way of peace.

Luke 1.68-79

DIVIDING BEAD

Jesus said, I am the true vine.
My Father is glorified by this, that you bear much fruit.

John 15.1a,8

Silence is kept.

5TH DECADE *A Song of the Church*

1 We praise you, O God, we acclaim you as the Lord; *
all creation worships you, the Father everlasting.

2 **To you all angels, all the powers of heaven,** *
the cherubim and seraphim, sing in endless praise:

3 Holy, holy, holy Lord, God of power and might,
heaven and earth are full of your glory.

4 **The glorious company of apostles praise you.**
The noble fellowship of prophets praise you. *
The white-robed army of martyrs praise you.

5 Throughout the world the holy Church acclaims you:
Father, of majesty unbounded, *
your true and only Son, worthy of all praise,
the Holy Spirit, advocate and guide.

6 **You, Christ, are the King of glory, ***
   the eternal Son of the Father.

7 When you took our flesh to set us free *
   you humbly chose the Virgin's womb.

8 **You overcame the sting of death ***
   and opened the kingdom of heaven to all believers.

9 You are seated at God's right hand in glory. *
   We believe that you will come and be our judge.

10 **Come then, Lord, and help your people,**
   bought with the price of your own blood, *
   and bring us with your saints to glory everlasting.

Te Deum Laudamus

DIVIDING BEAD

Holy, holy, holy, is the God of hosts;
who was, and who is, and who is to come.

Blessed be the creator of all things;
God in three persons:
the holy and undivided Trinity.

5TH BEAD

Almighty and everlasting God,
we thank you that you have brought us safely
to the beginning of this day.
Keep us from falling into sin
or running into danger,
order us in all our doings
and guide us to do always

what is righteous in your sight;
through Jesus Christ our Lord.
Amen.

TRIPLET OF BEADS

4 Awake, O sleeper, and arise from the dead,
    and Christ shall give you light.
  You have died and your life is hid with Christ in God.

3 Set your minds on things that are above,
    not on things that are on the earth.
  And Christ shall give you light.

2 When Christ our life appears you will appear with him in glory.
  **Awake, O sleeper, and arise from the dead,
  and Christ shall give you light.**

from Colossians 3

1ˢᵀ BEAD

Glory to God whose power, working in us,
can do infinitely more than we can ask or imagine:
Glory to him from generation to generation in the Church,
and in Christ Jesus for ever and ever.
Amen.

Ephesians 3.20,21

CROSS

May the God of hope fill us with all joy and peace
in believing through the power of the Holy Spirit.
Amen.

Let us bless the Lord.
Thanks be to God.

Prayer During the Day

CROSS

In the name of the Father and of the Son and of the Holy Spirit.
Amen.

The Lord's Prayer

As our Saviour taught us, so we pray
Our Father in heaven …

(or)

Let us pray with confidence as our Saviour has taught us
Our Father, who art in heaven …

The Apostles' Creed

I believe in God …

1ST BEAD

O God make speed to save us.
O Lord make haste to help us.

**Glory to the Father and to the Son
and to the Holy Spirit;
as it was in the beginning is now
and shall be for ever. Amen.**

TRIPLET OF BEADS

2 O Lord, you are our God: we call upon you all day long.
Lord, have mercy.

3 Rescue the weak and poor, deliver them from the power of
the wicked.
Christ, have mercy.

4 Lord, our souls wait for you, for our hope is in your word.
Lord, have mercy.

5TH BEAD

Blessed are you, Sovereign God, creator of all,
to you be glory and praise for ever.
You founded the earth in the beginning
and the heavens are the work of your hands.
In the fullness of time you made us in your image,
and in these last days you have spoken to us
in your Son Jesus Christ, the Word made flesh.
As we rejoice in the gift of your presence among us
let the light of your love always shine in our hearts,
your Spirit ever renew our lives
and your praises ever be on our lips.
Blessed be God, Father, Son and Holy Spirit.
Blessed be God for ever.

DIVIDING BEAD

The earth will be filled with the knowledge of the glory of the
Lord,
as the waters cover the sea.

Habakkuk 2.14

Silence is kept.

Before each decade begins, a prayer intention may be announced.
The cycle of intercession on pages 9–10 may be used.

IST DECADE   *A Song of God's Glorious Name*

1 O Lord our governor, *
   how glorious is your name in all the world!

2 **Your majesty above the heavens is praised ***
   out of the mouths of babes at the breast.

3 You have founded a stronghold against your foes, *
   that you might still the enemy and the avenger.

4 **When I consider your heavens, the work of your fingers, ***
   the moon and the stars that you have ordained,

5 What are mortals, that you should be mindful of them; *
   mere human beings, that you should seek them out?

6 **You have made them little lower than the angels ***
   and crown them with glory and honour.

7 You have given them dominion over the works of your hands *
   and put all things under their feet,

8 **All sheep and oxen, ***
   even the wild beasts of the field,

9 The birds of the air, the fish of the sea *
   and whatsoever walks in the paths of the sea.

10 **O Lord our governor, ***
   how glorious is your name in all the world!

Psalm 8

DIVIDING BEAD

Just as the body is one and has many members,
and all the members of the body, though many, are one body,
   so it is with Christ.
For in the one Spirit we were all baptized into one body.

I Corinthians 12.12,13a

Silence is kept.

2ND DECADE   *A Song of the Bride*

1 I will greatly rejoice in the Lord, *
   my soul shall exult in my God;

2 **Who has clothed me with the garments of salvation, ***
   and has covered me with the cloak of integrity,

3 As a bridegroom decks himself with a garland, *
   and as a bride adorns herself with her jewels.

4 **For as the earth puts forth her blossom, ***
   and as seeds in the garden spring up,

5 So shall God make righteousness and praise *
   blossom before all the nations.

6 **For Zion's sake I will not keep silent, ***
   and for Jerusalem's sake I will not rest,

7 Until her deliverance shines out like the dawn, *
   and her salvation as a burning torch.

8 **The nations shall see your deliverance, ***
   and all rulers shall see your glory;

9 Then you shall be called by a new name *
   which the mouth of God will give.

10 **You shall be a crown of glory in the hand of the Lord, ***
   a royal diadem in the hand of your God.

Isaiah 61.10,11; 62.1-3

DIVIDING BEAD

The love of Christ compels us.
We are ambassadors for him.

cf 2 Corinthians 5.14,20

Silence is kept.

3ᴿᴰ DECADE   *A Song of the Three*

1 Bless the Father, the Son and the Holy Spirit: *
   sing his praise and exalt him for ever.

2 **Bless the Lord all you works of the Lord: ***
   sing his praise and exalt him for ever.

3 Bless the Lord you heavens: *
   sing his praise and exalt him for ever.

4 **Bless the Lord you angels of the Lord: ***
   sing his praise and exalt him for ever.

5 Bless the Lord all people on earth: *
   sing his praise and exalt him for ever.

6 **O people of God bless the Lord: ***
   sing his praise and exalt him for ever.

7 Bless the Lord you priests of the Lord: *
  sing his praise and exalt him for ever.

8 **Bless the Lord you servants of the Lord: ***
  sing his praise and exalt him for ever.

9 Bless the Lord all you of upright spirit: *
  bless the Lord you that are holy and humble in heart.
                            The Song of the Three 35-37,60-65

10 **Bless the Father, the Son and the Holy Spirit: ***
   sing his praise and exalt him for ever.
   Benedicite – A Song of Creation (Shorter Version with Refrain)

DIVIDING BEAD

Jesus said, 'Come to me, all you that are weary and are carrying
heavy burdens, and I will give you rest.'

                                          Matthew 11.28

Silence is kept.

4ᵀᴴ DECADE   *A Song of Divine Love*

1 Love is patient and kind, love is not jealous or boastful,
     it is not arrogant or rude. *
  Love does not insist on its own way, it is not angry or resentful.

2 **It does not rejoice in wrongdoing ***
  but rejoices in the truth.

3 Love bears all things and believes all things; *
  love hopes all things and endures all things.

4 **Love will never come to an end, ***
  but prophecy will vanish,
  tongues cease and knowledge pass away.

5 Now we know only in part and we prophesy only in part, *
   But when the perfect comes, the partial shall pass away.

6 **When I was a child, I spoke like a child, ***
   I thought like a child, I reasoned like a child.

7 But when I became mature, *
   I put an end to childish ways.

8 **For now we see only puzzling reflections in a mirror, ***
   but then we will see face to face.

9 Now I know only in part; *
   then I shall know fully, even as I have been fully known.

10 **There are three things that last for ever, faith, hope**
      and love, *
   but the greatest of these is love.

1 Corinthians 13.4-13

DIVIDING BEAD

Jesus said, 'Love your enemies, do good to those who hate you,
bless those who curse you, pray for those who abuse you.'

Luke 6.27b,28

Silence is kept.

5ᵀᴴ DECADE   *The Ten Commandments*

1 Hear the commandments which God has given to his people,
      and examine your heart.
   I am the Lord your God: you shall have no other gods but me.
   Amen. Lord, have mercy.

2 You shall not make for yourself any idol.
   Amen. Lord, have mercy.

3 You shall not dishonour the name of the Lord your God.
   Amen. Lord, have mercy.

4 Remember the Sabbath and keep it holy.
   Amen. Lord, have mercy.

5 Honour your father and your mother.
   Amen. Lord, have mercy.

6 You shall not commit murder.
   Amen. Lord, have mercy.

7 You shall not commit adultery.
   Amen. Lord, have mercy.

8 You shall not steal.
   Amen. Lord, have mercy.

9 You shall not bear false witness against your neighbour.
   Amen. Lord, have mercy.

10 You shall not covet anything which belongs to your neighbour.
   Amen. Lord, have mercy upon us
   and write all these your laws in our hearts.

DIVIDING BEAD

Yours, Lord, is the greatness, the power,
the glory, the splendour and the majesty;
for everything in heaven and on earth is yours.

Yours, Lord, is the kingdom:
and you are exalted as head over all.

cf 1 Chronicles 29.11

5TH BEAD

O gracious and holy Father,
give us wisdom to perceive you,
diligence to seek you,
patience to wait for you,
eyes to behold you,
a heart to meditate upon you,
and a life to proclaim you,
through the power of the Spirit
of Jesus Christ our Lord.
Amen.

Benedict of Nursia (c.550)

TRIPLET OF BEADS

4 Jesus Christ is the light of the world,
   a light no darkness can quench.

3 The darkness is not dark to you,
   the night is as bright as the day.

2 Let your light scatter the darkness
   and fill your Church with your glory.

1ST BEAD

I bind unto myself today
the strong name of the Trinity,
by invocation of the same,
the Three in One, and One in Three.
Of whom all nature hath creation;
eternal Father, Spirit, Word:
Praise to the Lord of my salvation,
salvation is of Christ the Lord.

from St Patrick's Breastplate

CROSS

May Christ our redeemer bring us healing and wholeness.
Amen.

Let us bless the Lord.
Thanks be to God.

Evening Prayer

CROSS

In the name of the Father and of the Son and of the Holy Spirit.
Amen.

The Lord's Prayer

As our Saviour taught us, so we pray
Our Father in heaven …

(or)

Let us pray with confidence as our Saviour has taught us
Our Father, who art in heaven …

The Apostle's Creed

I believe in God …

1ST BEAD

O God make speed to save us.
O Lord make haste to help us.

**Glory to the Father and to the Son
and to the Holy Spirit;
as it was in the beginning is now
and shall be for ever. Amen.**

TRIPLET OF BEADS

2 O gladdening light,
  of the holy glory of the immortal Father
  heavenly, holy, blessed,
  O Jesus Christ.

3 Now that we have come to the setting of the sun
  and see the evening light
  we give praise to God,
  Father, Son and Holy Spirit.

4 Worthy are you at all times
  to be worshipped with holy voices,
  O Son of God and giver of life:
  therefore all the world glorifies you.

Phos Hilaron – a Song of the Light

5ᵀᴴ BEAD

Blessed are you, Lord God, creator of day and night:
to you be praise and glory for ever.
As darkness falls you renew your promise
to reveal among us the light of your presence.
By the light of Christ, your living Word,
dispel the darkness of our hearts
that we may walk as children of light
and sing your praise throughout the world.
Blessed be God, Father, Son and Holy Spirit.
Blessed be God for ever.

DIVIDING BEAD

I will give you as a light to the nations,
that my salvation may reach to the end of the earth.

Isaiah 49.6

Silence is kept.

Before each decade begins, a prayer intention may be announced.
The cycle of intercession on pages 9–10 may be used.

1ST DECADE

1 Bless the Lord, O my soul; *
   O Lord my God, how excellent is your greatness!

2 **You are clothed with majesty and honour, ***
   wrapped in light as in a garment.

3 The sun knows the time for its setting; *
   you make darkness that it may be night.

4 **O Lord, how manifold are your works! ***
   In wisdom you have made them all;
   the earth is full of your creatures.

5 All of these look to you *
   to give them their food in due season.

6 **When you send forth your spirit, they are created, ***
   and you renew the face of the earth.

7 May the glory of the Lord endure for ever; *
   may the Lord rejoice in all his works.

8 **I will sing to the Lord as long as I live; ***
   I will praise my God while I have my being.

9 So shall my song please him *
   while I rejoice in the Lord.

10 **Glory to the Father and to the Son and to the Holy Spirit; ***
   As it was in the beginning is now and shall be for ever. Amen.
   from Psalm 104

36

DIVIDING BEAD

'From the rising of the sun to its setting
my name is great among the nations,' says the Lord.

Malachi 1.11

Silence is kept.

2ᴺᴰ DECADE   *A Song of the Lord's Anointed*

1 The Spirit of the Lord is upon me *
  because he has anointed me.

2 **He has sent me to bring good news to the oppressed, ***
  to bind up the broken-hearted,

3 To proclaim liberty to the captives, *
  and the opening of the prison to those who are bound;

4 **To proclaim the year of the Lord's favour, ***
  to comfort all who mourn,

5 To give them a garland instead of ashes, *
  the oil of gladness instead of mourning,
      the mantle of praise instead of a faint spirit,

6 **That they may be called oaks of righteousness, ***
  the planting of the Lord, that he may be glorified.

7 For as the earth puts forth her blossom, *
  and as seeds in the garden spring up,

8 **So shall the Lord God make righteousness and praise ***
  blossom before all the nations.

9 You shall be called priests of the Lord; *
  they shall speak of you as ministers of our God.

Isaiah 61.1-3,11,6a

10 **Glory to the Father and to the Son and to the Holy Spirit; ***
   as it was in the beginning is now and shall be for ever. Amen.

DIVIDING BEAD

Jesus said, I am the light of the world.
Whoever follows me will have the light of life.

John 8.12

Silence is kept.

3ᴿᴰ DECADE   *A Song of the Justified*

1 God reckons as righteous those who believe, *
   who believe in him who raised Jesus from the dead;

2 **For Christ was handed over to death for our sins, ***
   and raised to life for our justification.

3 Since we are justified by faith, *
   we have peace with God through our Lord Jesus Christ.

4 **Through Christ we have gained access**
      to the grace in which we stand, *
   and rejoice in our hope of the glory of God.

5 We even exult in our sufferings, *
   for suffering produces endurance,

6 **And endurance brings hope, ***
   and our hope is not in vain,

7 Because God's love has been poured into our hearts, *
   through the Holy Spirit, given to us.

8 **God proves his love for us: ***
   while we were yet sinners Christ died for us.

9 Since we have been justified by his death, *
how much more shall we be saved from God's wrath.

10 **Therefore, we exult in God through our Lord Jesus Christ, ***
in whom we have now received our reconciliation.

Romans 4.24,25; 5.1-5,8,9,11

DIVIDING BEAD

The law was given through Moses;
grace and truth came through Jesus Christ.

John 1.17

Silence is kept.

4TH DECADE   *A Song of the Heavenly City*

1 By the river stood the tree of life, *
with healing for all the nations.

2 **I saw no temple in the city, ***
for its temple is the Lord God the Almighty and the Lamb.

3 And the city has no need of sun or moon to shine upon it, *
for the glory of God is its light, and its lamp is the Lamb.

4 **By its light the nations shall walk, ***
and the rulers of the earth shall bring their glory into it.

5 Its gates shall never be shut by day,
nor shall there be any night; *
they shall bring into it the glory and honour of the nations.

6 **I saw the river of the water of life, bright as crystal, ***
flowing from the throne of God and of the Lamb.

7 And either side of the river stood the tree of life,
yielding its fruit each month,*
and the leaves of the tree were for the healing of the nations.

8 **The throne of God and of the Lamb shall be there,**
   and his servants shall worship him; *
and they shall see God's face
   and his name shall be on their foreheads.

9 To the One who sits on the throne and to the Lamb *
be blessing and honour and glory and might,
for ever and ever. Amen.

10 **By the river stood the tree of life,** *
with healing for all the nations.

Revelation 21.22-26; 22.1,2b,d,3b,4
(vs. 1, 10 CW Refrain)

DIVIDING BEAD

For where two or three are gathered in my name,
I am there among them.

Matthew 18.20

Silence is kept.

5ᵀᴴ DECADE *The song of Mary*

1 My soul proclaims the greatness of the Lord, *
my spirit rejoices in God my Saviour,

2 **he has looked with favour on his lowly servant.** *
From this day all generations will call me blessed;

3 The Almighty has done great things for me *
and holy is his name.

4 **He has mercy on those who fear him,** *
from generation to generation.

5 He has shown strength with his arm *
and has scattered the proud in their conceit,

6 **Casting down the mighty from their thrones** *
   and lifting up the lowly.

7 He has filled the hungry with good things *
   and sent the rich away empty.

8 **He has come to the aid of his servant Israel,** *
   to remember his promise of mercy,

9 The promise made to our ancestors, *
   to Abraham and his children for ever.

10 **Glory to the Father and to the Son and to the Holy Spirit.** *
   as it was in the beginning is now and shall be for ever. Amen.

Luke 1.46-55

DIVIDING BEAD

O magnify the Lord with me;
let us exalt his name together.
O magnify the Lord with me;
let us exalt his name together.
I sought the Lord and he answered me;
he delivered me from all my fears.
O magnify the Lord with me.
In my weakness I cried to the Lord;
he heard me and saved me from my troubles.
Let us exalt his name together.

5TH BEAD

Lighten our darkness,
Lord, we pray,
and in your great mercy
defend us from all perils and dangers of this night,
for the love of your only Son,
our Saviour Jesus Christ.
Amen.

TRIPLET OF BEADS

4 Beloved, let us love one another, for love is of God;
  everyone who loves is born of God and knows God.
  Whoever does not love does not know God, for God is love.

3 In this the love of God was revealed among us,
  that God sent his only Son into the world,
    so that we might live through him.
  In this is love, not that we loved God but that he loved us,
  and sent his Son to be the expiation for our sins.

2 Beloved, since God loved us so much,
  we ought also to love one another.
  For if we love one another, God abides in us,
  and God's love will be perfected in us.

1 John 4.7-11,12b

IST BEAD

God be in my head, and in my understanding;
God be in my eyes, and in my looking;
God be in my mouth, and in my speaking;
God be in my heart, and in my thinking;
God be at mine end, and at my departing.
Amen.

Sarum Primer

CROSS

The grace of our Lord Jesus Christ, and the love of God,
and the fellowship of the Holy Spirit, be with us all ever more.
Amen.

Let us bless the Lord.
Thanks be to God.

Prayer at Night

CROSS

In the name of the Father and of the Son and of the Holy Spirit.
Amen.

The Lord's Prayer

As our Saviour taught us, so we pray
Our Father in heaven …

(or)

Let us pray with confidence as our Saviour has taught us
Our Father, who art in heaven …

The Apostles' Creed

I believe in God …

IST BEAD

The Lord almighty grant us a quiet night and a perfect end.
Amen.

Our help is in the name of the Lord:
Who made heaven and earth.

**Glory to the Father and to the Son
and to the Holy Spirit;
as it was in the beginning is now
and shall be for ever. Amen.**

TRIPLET OF BEADS

2 Christ has offered for all time a single sacrifice for sins.
He is seated at the right hand of God.

3 Through him let us offer up a sacrifice of praise to God:
the fruit of lips that acknowledge his name.

4 Do not forget to do good and share what you have.
Such sacrifices are pleasing to God.

5TH BEAD

A period of silence for reflection on the past day may follow.

Most merciful God, we confess to you,
before the whole company of heaven and one another,
that we have sinned in thought, word and deed
and in what we have failed to do.
Forgive us our sins, heal us by your Spirit
and raise us to new life in Christ. Amen.

DIVIDING BEAD

Into your hands, I commend my spirit.
For you have redeemed me, O Lord God of truth.

Psalm 31.5

Silence is kept.

Before each decade begins, a prayer intention may be announced.
The cycle of intercession on pages 9–10 may be used.

1ST DECADE

1 Come, bless the Lord, all you servants of the Lord, *
you that by night stand in the house of the Lord.

2 **Lift up your hands towards the sanctuary and bless the Lord.** *
The Lord who made heaven and earth
  give you blessing out of Zion.

Psalm 134

3 Answer me when I call, O God of my righteousness; *
you set me at liberty when I was in trouble;
have mercy on me and hear my prayer.

4 **How long will you nobles dishonour my glory;** *
how long will you love vain things and seek after falsehood?'

5 But know that the Lord has shown me his marvellous
    kindness; *
when I call upon the Lord, he will hear me.

6 **Stand in awe, and sin not;** *
commune with your own heart upon your bed, and be still.

7 Offer the sacrifices of righteousness *
and put your trust in the Lord.

8 **There are many that say, 'Who will show us any good?'** *
Lord, lift up the light of your countenance upon us.

9 You have put gladness in my heart,*
more than when corn and wine and oil increase.

10 **In peace I will lie down and sleep;** *
for it is you Lord, only, who make me dwell in safety.

Psalm 4

DIVIDING BEAD

You, O Lord, are in the midst of us and we are called by your
    name;
leave us not, O Lord our God.

Jeremiah 14.9

Silence is kept.

2ND DECADE

1 In you, O Lord, have I taken refuge;
      let me never be put to shame;
    deliver me in your righteousness. *
    Incline your ear to me; make haste to deliver me.

2 **Be my strong rock, a fortress to save me,**
    for you are my rock and my stronghold; *
    guide me, and lead me for your name's sake.

3 Into your hands I commend my spirit, *
    for you have redeemed me, O Lord God of truth.

4 **I will be glad and rejoice in your mercy, ***
    for you have seen my affliction and known my soul
        in adversity.

5 But my trust is in you, O Lord. *
    I have said, 'You are my God.

6 **'Make your face to shine upon your servant, ***
    and save me for your mercy's sake.'

7 How abundant is your goodness, O Lord,
    which you have laid up for those who fear you; *
    which you have prepared in the sight of all
    for those who put their trust in you.

8 **Blessed be the Lord! ***
    For he has shown me his steadfast love
    when I was as a city besieged.

9 Love the Lord, all you his servants; *
    for the Lord protects the faithful,
    but repays to the full the proud.

10 **Be strong and let your heart take courage,** *
   all you who wait in hope for the Lord.

Psalm 31.1-3,5,7,14,16,19,21,23,24

DIVIDING BEAD

Be sober, be vigilant, because your adversary the devil is prowling round like a roaring lion, seeking for someone to devour.
Resist him, strong in the faith.

1 Peter 5.8,9

Silence is kept.

3RD DECADE *A Song of Repentance*

1 Tell the good news of Jesus the Christ*
   to all who are searching for redemption.

2 **We declare to you what was from the beginning,** *
   what we have seen with our eyes and touched with our hands.

3 This is the message we have heard from Christ
      and proclaim to you: *
   that God is light, in whom there is no darkness at all.

4 **If we say that we have fellowship with God** *
   while we walk in darkness, we lie and do not do what is true.

5 But if we walk in the light as God is in the light, *
   we have fellowship with one another.

6 **And the blood of Jesus, the Son of God,** *
   cleanses us from all our sins.

7 If we say that we have no sin, *
   we deceive ourselves and the truth is not in us.

8 **If we confess our sins,** *
   the One who is faithful and just will forgive us
      and cleanse us from all unrighteousness.

9 Glory to the Father and to the Son and to the Holy Spirit; *
   as it was in the beginning is now and shall be for ever. Amen.

10 **Tell the good news of Jesus Christ** *
    to all who are searching for redemption.

1 John 1.1, 5-9
(vs. 1, 10 CW Refrain)

DIVIDING BEAD

The servants of the Lamb shall see the face of God, whose name
will be on their foreheads. There will be no more night: they will
not need the light of a lamp or the light of the sun, for God will be
their light, and they will reign for ever and ever.

Revelation 22.4,5

Silence is kept.

4ᵀᴴ DECADE   *A Song of the Blessed*

1 Blessed are the poor in spirit, *
   for theirs is the kingdom of heaven.

2 **Blessed are those who mourn,** *
   for they shall be comforted.

3 Blessed are the meek, *
   for they shall inherit the earth.

4 **Blessed are those who hunger**
      and thirst after righteousness, *
   for they shall be satisfied.

5 Blessed are the merciful, *
   for they shall obtain mercy.

6 **Blessed are the pure in heart,** *
for they shall see God.

7 Blessed are the peacemakers, *
for they shall be called the children of God.

8 **Blessed are those who suffer persecution for righteousness'**
   sake, *
for theirs is the kingdom of heaven.

9 Glory to the Father and to the Son and to the Holy Spirit; *
as it was in the beginning is now and shall be for ever. Amen.

10 **Rejoice and be glad for you are the light of the world,** *
   and great is your reward in heaven.

Matthew 5.3–10
(vs. 10 CW Refrain)

DIVIDING BEAD

Keep me as the apple of your eye;
Hide me under the shadow of your wings.

Psalm 17.8

Silence is kept.

5ᵀᴴ DECADE

1 Blessed are you, eternal God,
to be praised and glorified for ever.

2 Hear us as we pray for your holy catholic Church:
make us all one, that the world may believe.

3 Grant that every member of the Church
may truly and humbly serve you:
that the life of Christ may be revealed in us.

4 Strengthen all who minister in Christ's name:
   give them courage to proclaim your gospel.

5 Inspire and lead those who hold authority
   in the nations of the world:
   guide them in the ways of justice and peace.

6 Make us alive to the needs of our community:
   help us to share each other's joys and burdens.

7 Look with kindness on our homes and families:
   grant that your love may grow in our hearts.

8 Deepen our compassion for all who suffer from sickness,
      grief or trouble:
   in your presence may they find their strength.

9 We remember those who have died:
   Father, into your hands we commend them.

10 We praise you for all your saints who have entered
      your eternal glory:
   bring us all to share in your heavenly kingdom.

DIVIDING BEAD

Be present, O merciful God, and protect us through the silent
hours of this night, so that we who are wearied by the changes and
chances of this fleeting world, may rest upon your eternal
changelessness; through Jesus Christ our Lord.
Amen.

5ᵀᴴ BEAD

**Save us, O Lord, while waking,
and guard us while sleeping,
that awake we may watch with Christ,
and asleep may rest in peace.**

TRIPLET OF BEADS

4 Now, Lord, you let your servant go in peace:
your word has been fulfilled.

3 My own eyes have seen the salvation
which you have prepared in the sight of every people;

2 A light to reveal you to the nations
and the glory of your people Israel.

Luke 2.29–32

Glory to the Father and to the Son
and to the Holy Spirit;
as it was in the beginning is now
and shall be for ever. Amen.

1ˢᵀ BEAD

Save us, O Lord, while waking,
and guard us while sleeping,
that awake we may watch with Christ,
and asleep may rest in peace.

CROSS

In peace we will lie down and sleep;
for you alone, Lord, make us dwell in safety.
Abide with us, Lord Jesus,
for the night is at hand and the day is now past.
As the night watch looks for the morning,
so do we look for you, O Christ.

The Lord bless us and watch over us;
the Lord make his face shine upon us and be gracious to us;
the Lord look kindly on us and give us peace.
Amen.

Additional material for prayer during the week

The passages given for the triplet of beads can be used either in the opening or closing prayers on the stem of the rosary. The canticle for the day of the week can be used on any decade for any meditation and the collect may replace the prayer said on the fifth bead in the closing prayers.

A MORNING COLLECT

Almighty and everlasting God,
we thank you that you have brought us safely
to the beginning of this day.
Keep us from falling into sin
or running into danger,
order us in all our doings
and guide us to do always
what is righteous in your sight;
through Jesus Christ our Lord.
Amen.

A COLLECT THROUGH THE DAY

O God our protector,
by whose mercy the world turns safely into darkness
and returns again to light:
we give into your hands our unfinished tasks,
our unsolved problems,
and our unfulfilled hopes;

for you alone are our sure defence
and bring us lasting peace
in Jesus Christ our Lord.
Amen.

AN EVENING COLLECT

O God,
the source of all good desires,
all right judgements and all just works:
give to your servants that peace
which the world cannot give;
that our hearts may be set to obey your commandments,
and that, freed from the fear of our enemies,
we may pass our time in rest and quietness;
through Jesus Christ our Lord.
Amen.

SUNDAY

Triplet of Beads

The Lord is my light and my salvation;
the Lord is the strength of my life.
The Lord is my light and my salvation;
the Lord is the strength of my life.

The light shines in the darkness
and the darkness has not overcome it.
The Lord is the strength of my life.

Glory to the Father and to the Son
and to the Holy Spirit.
The Lord is my light and my salvation;
the Lord is the strength of my life.

from Psalm 27 and John 1

Canticle   *Benedicite – a Song of Creation*

1 Bless the Lord all you works of the Lord: *
   sing his praise and exalt him for ever.

2 **Bless the Lord you heavens: ***
   sing his praise and exalt him for ever.

3 Bless the Lord you angels of the Lord: bless the Lord all you
       his hosts; *
   bless the Lord you waters above the heavens:
   sing his praise and exalt him for ever.

4 **Bless the Lord sun and moon: bless the Lord you stars**
       of heaven; *
   bless the Lord all rain and dew:
   sing his praise and exalt him for ever.

5 Bless the Lord all winds that blow: bless the Lord you fire
       and heat; *
    bless the Lord scorching wind and bitter cold:
   sing his praise and exalt him for ever.

6 **O let the earth bless the Lord: bless the Lord you mountains**
       and hills; *
   bless the Lord all that grows in the ground:
   sing his praise and exalt him for ever.

7 Bless the Lord you springs: bless the Lord you seas and rivers; *
   bless the Lord you whales and all that swim in the waters:
   sing his praise and exalt him for ever.

8 **Bless the Lord all birds of the air: bless the Lord you beasts**
       and cattle; *
   bless the Lord all people on earth:
   sing his praise and exalt him for ever.

9 O people of God bless the Lord: bless the Lord you priests of the
  Lord; *
  bless the Lord you servants of the Lord:
  sing his praise and exalt him for ever.

10 **Bless the Lord all you of upright spirit:**
   bless the Lord you that are holy and humble in heart; *
   bless the Father, the Son and the Holy Spirit:
   sing his praise and exalt him for ever.

The Song of the Three 35-65

Collect

God of glory,
by the raising of your Son
you have broken the chains of death and hell:
fill your Church with faith and hope;
for a new day has dawned
and the way to life stands open
in our Saviour Jesus Christ.
Amen.

MONDAY

Triplet of Beads

Trust in the Lord with all your heart;
and be not wise in your own sight.
Trust in the Lord with all your heart;
and be not wise in your own sight.

In all your ways acknowledge him
and he will make straight your paths.
Trust in the Lord with all your heart.

Glory to the Father and to the Son
and to the Holy Spirit.

Trust in the Lord with all your heart;
and be not wise in your own sight.

from Proverbs 3

Canticle   *A song of Deliverance*

1 All the earth, shout and sing for joy, *
   for great in your midst is the Holy One.

2 **'Behold, God is my salvation; ***
   I will trust and will not be afraid;

3 'For the Lord God is my strength and my song, *
   and has become my salvation.'

4 **With joy you will draw water ***
   from the wells of salvation.

5 On that day you will say, *
   'Give thanks to the Lord, call upon his name;

6 **'Make known his deeds among the nations, ***
   proclaim that his name is exalted.

7 'Sing God's praises, who has triumphed gloriously; *
   let this be known in all the world.

8 **'Shout and sing for joy, you that dwell in Zion, ***
   for great in your midst is the Holy One of Israel.'

Isaiah 12.2-6

9 Glory to the Father and to the Son and to the Holy Spirit; *
   as it was in the beginning is now and shall be for ever. Amen.

10 **All the earth, shout and sing for joy, ***
    for great in your midst is the Holy One.

(vs. 1,10 CW Refrain)

Collect

Kindle in our hearts, O God,
the flame of love which never ceases,
that it may burn in us, giving light to others.
May we shine for ever in your temple,
set on fire with your eternal light,
even your Son Jesus Christ,
our Saviour and our Redeemer.
Amen.

TUESDAY

Triplet of Beads

Open my eyes, O Lord
that I may see the wonders of your law.
Open my eyes, O Lord
that I may see the wonders of your law.

Lead me in the path of your commandments
that I may see the wonders of your law.

Glory to the Father and to the Son
and to the Holy Spirit.
Open my eyes, O Lord
that I may see the wonders of your law.

from Psalm 119

Canticle   *A Song of Trust*

1 We have a strong city; he sets up salvation as walls and
     bulwarks. *
   Open the gates, that the righteous nation which keeps faith
     may enter in.

2 **You will keep him in perfect peace, whose mind is stayed on
    you,** *
  because he trusts in you.

3 Trust in the Lord for ever, *
  for the Lord God is an everlasting rock.

4 **The way of the righteous is level;** *
  you who are upright make smooth the path of the righteous.

5 In the path of your judgements, O Lord, we wait for you; *
  your name and renown is the desire of our soul.

6 **My soul yearns for you in the night,** *
  my spirit within me earnestly seeks you.

7 For when your judgements are in the earth, *
  the inhabitants of the world learn righteousness.

8 **O Lord, you will ordain peace for us,** *
  for indeed all that we have done you have done for us.

Isaiah 26.1-4,7-9,12

9 Glory to the Father and to the Son and to the Holy Spirit; *
  as it was in the beginning is now and shall be for ever. Amen.

10 **Trust in the Lord for ever,** *
   for the Lord God is an everlasting rock.

(vs.10 CW Refrain)

Collect

Eternal God and Father,
you create and redeem us by the power of your love:
guide and strengthen us by your Spirit,
that we may give ourselves in love and service

to one another and to you;
through Jesus Christ our Lord.
Amen.

WEDNESDAY

Triplet of Beads

Lord, you will guide me with your counsel
and afterwards receive me with glory.
**Lord, you will guide me with your counsel
and afterwards receive me with glory.**

For I am always with you;
you hold me by my right hand.
And afterwards receive me with glory.

Glory to the Father and to the Son
and to the Holy Spirit.
**Lord, you will guide me with your counsel
and afterwards receive me with glory.**

from Psalm 73

Canticle   *A Song of Hannah*

1 My heart exults in the Lord; my strength is exalted in my God. *
    My mouth derides my enemies, because I rejoice in your
        salvation.

2 **There is no Holy One like you, O Lord, ***
    nor any Rock like you, our God.

3 For you are a God of knowledge *
    and by you our actions are weighed.

4 **The bows of the mighty are broken, ***
    but the feeble gird on strength.

5 Those who were full now hire themselves out for bread, *
  but those who were hungry are well fed.

6 **The barren woman has borne sevenfold, ***
  but she who has many children is forlorn.

7 Both the poor and the rich are of your making; *
  you bring low and you also exalt.

8 **You raise up the poor from the dust, ***
  and lift the needy from the ash heap.

9 You make them sit with the rulers *
  and inherit a place of honour.

10 **For the pillars of the earth are yours ***
   and on them you have set the world.

1 Samuel 2.1,2,3b-5,7,8

Collect

Eternal Lord,
our beginning and our end:
bring us with the whole creation
to your glory, hidden through past ages
and made known
in Jesus Christ our Lord.
Amen.

THURSDAY

Triplet of Beads

Fear not, for I have redeemed you.
I have called you by name; you are mine.
Fear not, for I have redeemed you.
I have called you by name; you are mine.

When you pass through the waters, I will be with you.
When you walk through fire, you shall not be burned.
I have called you by name; you are mine.

Glory to the Father and to the Son
and to the Holy Spirit.
Fear not, for I have redeemed you.
I have called you by name; you are mine.

from Isaiah 43

Canticle   *A Song of God's Descending*

1 I love you, O Lord my strength. *
    The Lord is my crag, my fortress and my deliverer.

2 **In my distress I called upon the Lord**
    and cried out to my God for help. *
    He heard my voice in his temple and my cry came to his ears.

3 He parted the heavens and came down *
    and thick darkness was under his feet.

4 **He rode upon the cherubim and flew; ***
    he came flying on the wings of the wind.

5 He made darkness his covering round about him, *
    dark waters and thick clouds his pavilion.

6 **From the brightness of his presence, through the clouds ***
    burst hailstones and coals of fire.

7 The Lord also thundered out of heaven; *
    the Most High uttered his voice with hailstones and coals of fire.

8 **For you will save a lowly people ***
    and bring down the high looks of the proud.

9 You also shall light my candle; *
   the Lord my God shall make my darkness to be bright.

10 **As for God, his way is perfect;**
   the word of the Lord is tried in the fire; *
   he is a shield to all who trust in him.

Psalm 18.1,6,7,10-14,28,29,31

Collect

O God, the author of peace
and lover of concord,
to know you is eternal life,
to serve you is perfect freedom.
Defend us your servants
from all assaults of our enemies;
that we, surely trusting in your defence,
may not fear the power of any adversaries;
through Jesus Christ our Lord.
Amen.

FRIDAY

Triplet of Beads

Forsake me not, O Lord;
be not far from me, O my God.
Forsake me not, O Lord;
be not far from me, O my God.

Make haste to help me,
O Lord of my salvation.
Be not far from me, O my God.

Glory to the Father and to the Son
and to the Holy Spirit.

Forsake me not, O Lord;
be not far from me, O my God.

from Psalm 38

Canticle   *A Song of God's Compassion*

1 The Lord is full of compassion and mercy, *
  slow to anger and of great kindness.

2 **He will not always accuse us, ***
  neither will he keep his anger for ever.

3 He has not dealt with us according to our sins, *
  nor rewarded us according to our wickedness.

4 **For as the heavens are high above the earth, ***
  so great is his mercy upon those who fear him.

5 As far as the east is from the west, *
  so far has he set our sins from us.

6 **As a father has compassion on his children, ***
  so is the Lord merciful towards those who fear him.

7 For he knows of what we are made; *
  he remembers that we are but dust.

8 **Our days are but as grass; we flourish as a flower of the field; ***
  For as soon as the wind goes over it, it is gone,
  and its place shall know it no more.

9 But the merciful goodness of the Lord is from of old
  and endures for ever on those who fear him, *
  and his righteousness on children's children;

10 **On those who keep his covenant ***
   and remember his commandments to do them.

Psalm 103.8-18

Collect

Gracious Father,
you gave up your Son
out of love for the world:
lead us to ponder the mysteries of his passion,
that we may know eternal peace
through the shedding of our Saviour's blood,
Jesus Christ our Lord.
Amen.

SATURDAY

Triplet of Beads

Your salvation is near to those who fear you;
that glory may dwell in our land.
Your salvation is near to those who fear you;
that glory may dwell in our land.

Mercy and truth have met together;
righteousness and peace have kissed each other.
That glory may dwell in our land.

Glory to the Father and to the Son
and to the Holy Spirit.
Your salvation is near to those who fear you;
that glory may dwell in our land.

from Psalm 85

Canticle

1 The Lord is my light and my salvation; whom then shall I fear? *
   The Lord is the strength of my life; of whom then shall I be afraid?

2 **Though a host encamp against me,**
     my heart shall not be afraid, *

and though there rise up war against me,
    yet will I put my trust in him.

3 One thing have I asked of the Lord and that alone I seek: *
    that I may dwell in the house of the Lord all the days of my life,

4 **To behold the fair beauty of the Lord ***
    and to seek his will in his temple.

5 For in the day of trouble he shall hide me in his shelter; *
    in the secret place of his dwelling shall he hide me
       and set me high upon a rock.

6 **Therefore will I offer in his dwelling an oblation**
      with great gladness; *
    I will sing and make music to the Lord.

7 Hear my voice, O Lord, when I call; *
    have mercy upon me and answer me.

8 **My heart tells of your word, 'Seek my face.' ***
    Your face, Lord, will I seek.

9 I believe that I shall see the goodness of the Lord *
    in the land of the living.

10 **Wait for the Lord; be strong and he shall comfort your heart; ***
    wait patiently for the Lord.

Psalm 27.1,3-6,8-10,16-17

Collect

Grant, Lord,
that we who are baptized into the death
of your Son our Saviour Jesus Christ
may continually put to death our evil desires
and be buried with him;

and that through the grave and gate of death
we may pass to our joyful resurrection;
through his merits,
who died and was buried and rose again for us,
your Son Jesus Christ our Lord.
Amen.

Part Two: Seasonal Prayers with the Rosary

Advent

CROSS

In the name of the Father and of the Son and of the Holy Spirit.
Amen.

The Lord's Prayer

Awaiting his coming in glory,
as our Saviour taught us, so we pray
Our Father in heaven …

(or)

Awaiting his coming in glory,
    let us pray with confidence as our Saviour has taught us
Our Father, who art in heaven …

The Apostles' Creed

I believe in God …

1ST BEAD

O God, make speed to save us.
O Lord, make haste to help us.

Reveal among us the light of your presence
that we may behold your power and glory.

Glory to the Father and to the Son
and to the Holy Spirit;
as it was in the beginning is now
and shall be for ever. Amen.

TRIPLET OF BEADS

2 My soul is waiting for you, O Lord:
in your word is my hope.
My soul is waiting for you, O Lord:
in your word is my hope.

3 There is forgiveness with you,
so that you shall be feared.
In your word is my hope.

4 Glory to the Father and to the Son
and to the Holy Spirit.
My soul is waiting for you, O Lord:
in your word is my hope.

from Psalm 130

5TH BEAD

Blessed are you, Sovereign God of all,
to you be praise and glory for ever.
In your tender compassion
the dawn from on high is breaking upon us
to dispel the lingering shadows of night.
Open our eyes to behold your presence
and strengthen our hands to do your will,
that the world may rejoice and give you praise.
Blessed be God, Father, Son and Holy Spirit.
Blessed be God for ever.

DIVIDING BEAD

The Advent Antiphons are said on the Dividing Beads.

O Wisdom, coming forth from the mouth of the Most High,
reaching from one end to the other mightily,
and sweetly ordering all things:
Come and teach us the way of prudence.

cf Ecclesiasticus 24.3; Wisdom 8.1

Silence is kept.

Before each decade begins, a prayer intention may be announced.
The cycle of intercession on pages 10–12 may be used.

1ST DECADE   *A Song of the King's Glory*

1 The earth is the Lord's and all that fills it, *
   the compass of the world and all who dwell therein.

2 **For he has founded it upon the seas ***
   and set it firm upon the rivers of the deep.

3 'Who shall ascend the hill of the Lord, *
   or who can rise up in his holy place?'

4 **'Those who have clean hands and a pure heart, ***
   who have not lifted up their soul to an idol,
     nor sworn an oath to a lie;

5 'They shall receive a blessing from the Lord, *
   a just reward from the God of their salvation.'

6 **Such is the company of those who seek him, ***
   of those who seek your face, O God of Jacob.

7 Lift up your heads, O gates; be lifted up, you everlasting doors; *
   and the King of glory shall come in.

8 'Who is the King of glory?' *
   'The Lord, strong and mighty,
      the Lord who is mighty in battle.'

9 Lift up your heads, O gates; be lifted up, you everlasting doors; *
   and the King of glory shall come in.

10 'Who is this King of glory?' *
   'The Lord of hosts, he is the King of glory.'

Psalm 24

DIVIDING BEAD

O Adonai, and leader of the House of Israel,
who appeared to Moses in the fire of the burning bush
and gave him the law on Sinai:
Come and redeem us with an outstretched arm.

cf Exodus 3.2; 24.12

Silence is kept.

2ND DECADE   *A Song of the Wilderness*

1 Lift up your voice with strength, *
   O herald of good tidings.

2 **The wilderness and the dry land shall rejoice, ***
   the desert shall blossom and burst into song.

3 They shall see the glory of the Lord, *
   the majesty of our God.

4 **Strengthen the weary hands, ***
   and make firm the feeble knees.

5 Say to the anxious, 'Be strong, fear not,
      your God is coming with judgement, *
   coming with judgement to save you.'

6 **Then shall the eyes of the blind be opened, ***
   and the ears of the deaf unstopped;

7 Then shall the lame leap like a hart,*
   and the tongue of the dumb sing for joy.

8 **For waters shall break forth in the wilderness, ***
   and streams in the desert;

9 The ransomed of the Lord shall return with singing, *
   with everlasting joy upon their heads.

10 **Joy and gladness shall be theirs, ***
   and sorrow and sighing shall flee away.

Isaiah 35.1,2b-4a,4c-6,10
(vs. 1 CW Refrain)

DIVIDING BEAD

O Root of Jesse, standing as a sign among the peoples;
before you kings will shut their mouths,
to you the nations will make their prayer:
Come and deliver us, and delay no longer.

cf Isaiah 11.10; 45.14; 52.15; Romans 15.12

Silence is kept.

3ᴿᴰ DECADE   *A Song of the Spirit*

1 Surely I am coming soon. *
   Amen. Come, Lord Jesus!

2 **'Behold, I am coming soon', says the Lord,**
   and bringing my reward with me, *
   to give to everyone according to their deeds.

3 'I am the Alpha and the Omega, the first and the last, *
   the beginning and the end.'

4 **Blessed are those who do God's commandments, ***
   that they may have the right to the tree of life,
   and may enter into the city through the gates.

5 'I have sent my angel to you, *
   with this testimony for all the churches.

6 **'I am the root and the offspring of David, ***
   I am the bright morning star.'

7 'Come!' say the Spirit and the Bride; *
   'Come!' let each hearer reply!

8 **Come forward, you who are thirsty, ***
   let those who desire take the water of life as a gift.

9 To the One who sits on the throne and to the Lamb *
   Be blessing and honour and glory and might,
      for ever and ever. Amen.

10 **Surely I am coming soon. ***
   Amen. Come, Lord Jesus!

Revelation 22.12-14,16,17
(vs. 1, 10 CW Refrain)

DIVIDING BEAD

O Key of David and sceptre of the House of Israel;
you open and no one can shut; you shut and no one can open:
Come and lead the prisoners from the prison house,
those who dwell in darkness and the shadow of death.

cf Isaiah 22.22; 42.7

Silence is kept.

4TH DECADE   *The Advent Prose*

1 Pour down, O heavens, from above, *
   and let the skies rain down righteousness.

2 **Turn your fierce anger from us, O Lord,** *
  and remember not our sins for ever.

3 Your holy cities have become a desert,
  Zion a wilderness, Jerusalem a desolation; *
  our holy and beautiful house, where our ancestors praised you.

4 **We have sinned and become like one who is unclean;**
  we have all withered like a leaf, *
  and our iniquities like the wind have swept us away.

5 You have hidden your face from us, *
   and abandoned us to our iniquities.

6 **You are my witnesses, says the Lord,**
  and my servant whom I have chosen, *
  that you may know me and believe me.

7 I myself am the Lord, and none but I can deliver; *
  what my hand holds, none can snatch away.

8 **Comfort my people, comfort them;** *
  my salvation shall not be delayed.

9 I have swept your offences away like a cloud;
     fear not, for I will save you. *
  I am the Lord your God, the Holy One of Israel, your redeemer.

10 **Pour down, O heavens, from above,** *
   and let the skies rain down righteousness.

DIVIDING BEAD

O Morning Star,
splendour of light eternal and sun of righteousness:
Come and enlighten those who dwell in darkness
   and the shadow of death.

cf Malachi 4.2

Silence is kept.

5ᵀᴴ DECADE   *The Song of Zechariah*

1 Blessed be the Lord, the God of Israel, *
  who has come to his people and set them free.

2 **He has raised up for us a mighty Saviour, ***
  born of the house of his servant, David.

3 Through his holy prophets, God promised of old *
  to save us from our enemies,
    from the hands of all that hate us.

4 **To show mercy to our ancestors, ***
  and to remember his holy covenant.

5 This was the oath God swore to our father Abraham: *
  to set us free from the hands of our enemies,

6 **Free to worship him without fear, ***
  holy and righteous in his sight, all the days of our life.

7 And you, child, shall be called the prophet of the Most High, *
  for you will go before the Lord to prepare his way,

8 **To give his people knowledge of salvation ***
  by the forgiveness of all their sins.

9 In the tender compassion of our God *
  the dawn from on high shall break upon us,

10 **To shine on those who dwell in darkness**
     and the shadow of death, *
   and to guide our feet into the way of peace.

Luke 1.68-79

DIVIDING BEAD

O King of the nations, and their desire,
the cornerstone making both one:
**Come and save the human race,
which you fashioned from clay.**

cf Isaiah 28.16; Ephesians 2.14

5TH BEAD

Almighty God,
give us grace to cast away the works of darkness
and to put on the armour of light,
now in the time of this mortal life,
in which your Son Jesus Christ came to us in great humility;
that on the last day,
when he shall come again in his glorious majesty
to judge the living and the dead,
we may rise to the life immortal;
through him who is alive and reigns with you,
in the unity of the Holy Spirit,
one God, now and for ever.
Amen.

TRIPLET OF BEADS

4 Saviour eternal, life of the world unfailing,
   light everlasting and our true redemption.

3 Taking our humanity in your loving freedom,
   you rescued our lost earth and filled the world with joy.

2 By your first advent justify us, by your second, set us free:
   that when the great light dawns and you come as judge of all,
   we may be robed in immortality
   **and ready, Lord, to follow
   in your footsteps blest, wherever they may lead.**

after the Advent Sequence

1ST BEAD

O Emmanuel, our King and our lawgiver,
the hope of the nations and their Saviour:
Come and save us, O Lord our God.

cf Isaiah 7.14

CROSS

May the Lord, when he comes, find us watching and waiting.
Amen.

Let us bless the Lord.
Thanks be to God.

Christmas

CROSS

In the name of the Father and of the Son and of the Holy Spirit.
Amen.

The Lord's Prayer

Rejoicing in the presence of God here among us,
as our Saviour taught us, so we pray
Our Father in heaven …

(or)

Rejoicing in the presence of God here among us,
let us pray with confidence as our Saviour has taught us
Our Father, who art in heaven …

The Apostles' Creed

I believe in God …

1ST BEAD

O God make speed to save us.
O Lord make haste to help us.

You laid the foundation of the earth
and the heavens are the work of your hands.

**Glory to the Father and to the Son
and to the Holy Spirit;
as it was in the beginning is now
and shall be for ever. Amen.**

TRIPLET OF BEADS

2 The Word of life which was from the beginning we proclaim
    to you.
    **The darkness is passing away and the true light is already
    shining;**

3 That which we heard, which we saw with our eyes,
        and touched with our hands,
    we proclaim to you.

4 For our fellowship is with the Father, and with his Son,
        Jesus Christ our Lord.
    **The Word of life which was from the beginning we proclaim
    to you.**

from 1 John 1

5TH BEAD

Blessed are you, sovereign God,
creator of heaven and earth,
to you be praise and glory for ever.
As your living Word, eternal in heaven,
assumed the frailty of our mortal flesh,
may the light of your love be born in us
to fill our hearts with joy as we sing:
Blessed be God, Father, Son and Holy Spirit.
Blessed be God for ever.

DIVIDING BEAD

Welcome all wonders in one sight!
Eternity shut in a span.
Summer in winter, day in night,
heaven in earth and God in man.
Great little one whose all-embracing birth
brings earth to heaven, stoops heaven to earth.

Silence is kept.

Before each decade begins, a prayer intention may be announced.
The cycle of intercession on pages 10–12 may be used.

1ST DECADE

1 When peaceful silence lay over all,
   and night was in the midst of her swift course: *
   from your royal throne, O God, down from the heavens,
   leapt your almighty Word.

2 **Alleluia. Give praise, you servants of the Lord, ***
   O praise the name of the Lord.

3 Blessed be the name of the Lord, *
   from this time forth and for evermore.

4 **From the rising of the sun to its setting ***
   let the name of the Lord be praised.

5 The Lord is high above all nations *
   and his glory above the heavens.

6 **Who is like the Lord our God, that has his throne so high, ***
   yet humbles himself to behold the things of heaven and earth?

7 He raises the poor from the dust *
   and lifts the needy from the ashes,

8 **To set them with princes, ***
   with the princes of his people.

9 He gives the barren woman a place in the house *
   and makes her a joyful mother of children. Alleluia.

Psalm 113

10 **When peaceful silence lay over all,**
   and night was in the midst of her swift course: *
   from your royal throne, O God, down from the heavens,
   leapt your almighty Word.
      (vs. 1,10 CW Refrain for the Benedictus in Christmas Season)

DIVIDING BEAD

The shepherds said to one another,
'Let us go now to Bethlehem
and see this thing that has taken place,
which the Lord has made known to us.'

Luke 2.15

Silence is kept.

2ND DECADE *A Song of the Messiah*

1 To us a child is born, *
   to us a son is given.

2 **The people who walked in darkness have seen a great light; ***
   those who dwelt in a land of deep darkness,
      upon them the light has dawned.

3 You have increased their joy and given them great gladness; *
   they rejoiced before you as with joy at the harvest.

4 **For you have shattered the yoke that burdened them; ***
   the collar that lay heavy on their shoulders.

5 For to us a child is born and to us a son is given, *
 and the government will be upon his shoulder.

6 **And his name will be called: Wonderful Counsellor,**
  the Mighty God; *
 the Everlasting Father, the Prince of Peace.

7 Of the increase of his government and of peace *
 there will be no end,

8 **Upon the throne of David and over his kingdom, ***
 to establish and uphold it with justice and righteousness.

9 From this time forth and for evermore; *
 the zeal of the Lord of hosts will do this.

10 **Glory to the Father and to the Son and to the Holy Spirit; ***
  as it was in the beginning is now and shall be for ever. Amen.

Isaiah 9: 2,3b,4a,6,7
(vs. 1 CW Refrain)

DIVIDING BEAD

To us is born a Saviour, who is Christ the Lord,
and all the heavenly hosts now sing,
Glory to God in the highest.

Silence is kept.

3ʀᴅ DECADE *A Song of God's Chosen One*

1 To us is born a Saviour, who is Christ the Lord, *
 and all the heavenly hosts now sing, Glory to God in the highest.

2 **There shall come forth a shoot from the stock of Jesse, ***
 and a branch shall grow out of his roots.

3 And the Spirit of the Lord shall rest upon him, *
the spirit of wisdom and understanding,

4 **The spirit of counsel and might, ***
the spirit of knowledge and the fear of the Lord.

5 He shall not judge by what his eyes see, *
or decide by what his ears hear,

6 **But with righteousness he shall judge the poor, ***
and decide with equity for the meek of the earth.

7 The wolf shall dwell with the lamb, *
and the leopard shall lie down with the kid.

8 **The calf, the lion and the fatling together, ***
with a little child to lead them.

9 They shall not hurt or destroy in all my holy mountain, *
for the earth shall be full of the knowledge of the Lord
as the waters cover the sea.

10 **Glory to the Father and to the Son and to the Holy Spirit; ***
as it was in the beginning is now and shall be for ever. Amen.

Isaiah 11.1,2,3b-4a,6,9
(vs. 1 CW Refrain for the Benedictus in Christmas Season)

DIVIDING BEAD

A voice from heaven said, 'This is my Son, the Beloved,
with whom I am well pleased.'

Matthew 3.17

Silence is kept.

4TH DECADE *A Song of God's Grace*

1 Blessed are you, the God and Father of our Lord Jesus Christ, *
for you have blest us in Christ Jesus
   with every spiritual blessing in the heavenly places.

2 **You chose us to be yours in
Christ before the foundation of the world, *
that we should be holy and blameless before you.**

3 In love you destined us for adoption as your children,
   through Jesus Christ, *
according to the purpose of your will,

4 **To the praise of your glorious grace, *
which you freely bestowed on us in the Beloved.**

5 In you, we have redemption through the blood of Christ, *
the forgiveness of our sins,

6 **According to the riches of your grace, *
which you have lavished upon us.**

7 You have made known to us, in all wisdom and insight, *
the mystery of your will,

8 **According to your purpose which you set forth in Christ, *
as a plan for the fullness of time,**

9 To unite all things in Christ, *
things in heaven and things on earth.

Ephesians 1.3-10

10 **Glory to the Father and to the Son and to the Holy Spirit; *
as it was in the beginning is now and shall be for ever. Amen.**

DIVIDING BEAD

I am bringing you good news of great joy for all the people:
**to you is born this day in the city of David a Saviour,
  who is Christ, the Lord.**

Luke 2.10,11

Silence is kept.

5TH DECADE

1 Blessed are you, God of all glory, through your Son the Christ.
His name is Jesus because he saves his people from their sin.
He will be called Emmanuel:
 God is with us.

2 Let us praise the Lord, the God of Israel:
he has come to his people and set them free.

3 He gave up the glory of heaven
and took the form of a servant.

4 The Word was made flesh
and we beheld his glory.

5 In humility he walked the path of obedience
to die on the cross.

6 God raised him to the highest place above
and gave him the name above every name:
Jesus Christ is Lord.

7 So all beings in heaven and earth will fall at his feet,
and proclaim to the glory of God:
Jesus Christ is Lord.

8 Jesus Christ is the light of the world;
Jesus is our Way.

9 With Jesus even dark places are light;
   Jesus is the Truth.

10 In Jesus we shall live for ever;
    Jesus is our Life.

DIVIDING BEAD

Hear the words of Saint John:
God's love for us was revealed when God sent his only Son into
   the world
so that we could have life through him.
Thanks be to God.

5ᵀᴴ BEAD

Almighty God,
who wonderfully created us in your own image
and yet more wonderfully restored us
through your Son Jesus Christ:
grant that, as he came to share our humanity,
so we may share the life of his divinity;
who is alive and reigns with you,
in the unity of the Holy Spirit,
one God, now and for ever.
Amen.

TRIPLET OF BEADS

4 The Word became flesh and dwelt among us,
   full of grace and truth.
   The Word became flesh and dwelt among us,
   full of grace and truth.

3 And we have seen his glory, the glory as of a father's only son,
   full of grace and truth.

2 Glory to the Father and to the Son and to the Holy Spirit.
The Word became flesh and dwelt among us,
full of grace and truth.

from John 1

1ST BEAD

Christ Jesus was in the form of God,
but he did not cling to equality with God.
He emptied himself, taking the form of a servant,
and was born in our human likeness.
Being found in human form he humbled himself,
and became obedient unto death, even death on a cross.
Therefore God has highly exalted him,
and bestowed on him the name above every name,
That at the name of Jesus every knee should bow,
in heaven and on earth and under the earth;
And every tongue confess that Jesus Christ is Lord,
to the glory of God the Father.

Philippians 2.5-11

CROSS

May God, who has called us out of darkness
into his marvellous light, bless us and fill us with peace.
Amen.

Let us bless the Lord.
Thanks be to God.

Epiphany

CROSS

In the name of the Father and of the Son and of the Holy Spirit.
Amen.

The Lord's Prayer

Believing the promises of God,
as our Saviour taught us, so we pray
Our Father in heaven…

(or)

Believing the promises of God,
let us pray with confidence as our Saviour has taught us
Our Father, who art in heaven …

The Apostles' Creed

I believe in God …

1ST BEAD

O God, make speed to save us.
O Lord, make haste to help us.

From the rising of the sun to its setting
your glory is proclaimed in all the world.

**Glory to the Father and to the Son
and to the Holy Spirit;
as it was in the beginning is now
and shall be for ever. Amen.**

TRIPLET OF BEADS

2 Lord Jesus, illuminate the darkness in our hearts:
   Lord, have mercy.
   Lord, have mercy.

3 Lord Jesus, open our eyes to your saving love:
   Christ, have mercy.
   Christ, have mercy.

4 Lord Jesus, unstop our ears to hear your living word:
   Lord, have mercy.
   Lord, have mercy.

5TH BEAD

Blessed are you, Sovereign God,
our light and our salvation,
to you be glory and praise for ever.
You gave your Christ as a light to the nations,
and through the anointing of the Spirit
you established us as a royal priesthood.
As you call us into your marvellous light,
may our lives bear witness to your truth
and our lips never cease to proclaim your praise.
Blessed be God, Father, Son and Holy Spirit.
Blessed be God for ever.

DIVIDING BEAD

The grace of God has appeared,
bringing salvation to all.

Titus 2.11

Silence is kept.

Before each decade begins, a prayer intention may be announced.
The cycle of intercession on pages 10–12 may be used.

1ST DECADE

1 Give the king your judgements, O God, *
and your righteousness to the son of a king.

2 **The kings of Tarshish and of the isles shall pay tribute; ***
the kings of Sheba and Seba shall bring gifts.

3 All kings shall fall down before him; *
all nations shall do him service.

4 **For he shall deliver the poor that cry out, ***
the needy and those who have no helper.

5 He shall have pity on the weak and poor; *
he shall preserve the lives of the needy.

6 **He shall redeem their lives from oppression and violence, ***
and dear shall their blood be in his sight.

7 Long may he live; unto him may be given gold from Sheba; *
may prayer be made for him continually
and may they bless him all the day long.

8 **May there be abundance of grain on the earth,**
standing thick upon the hilltops; *
may its fruit flourish like Lebanon
and its grain grow like the grass of the field.

9 May his name remain for ever
        and be established as long as the sun endures; *
    may all nations be blest in him and call him blessed.

10 **Blessed be the Lord, the God of Israel,**
    who alone does wonderful things. *
    And blessed be his glorious name for ever.
    May all the earth be filled with his glory. Amen. Amen.

Psalm 72.1,10-19

DIVIDING BEAD

We do not proclaim ourselves;
we proclaim Jesus Christ as Lord
and ourselves as your slaves for Jesus' sake.

2 Corinthians 4.5

Silence is kept.

2ND DECADE

1 Ascribe to the Lord, you powers of heaven, *
    ascribe to the Lord glory and strength.

2 **Ascribe to the Lord the honour due to his name; ***
    worship the Lord in the beauty of holiness.

3 The voice of the Lord is upon the waters;
        the God of glory thunders; *
    the Lord is upon the mighty waters.

4 **The voice of the Lord is mighty in operation; ***
    the voice of the Lord is a glorious voice.

5 The voice of the Lord breaks the cedar trees; *
    the Lord breaks the cedars of Lebanon;

6 **He makes Lebanon skip like a calf ***
    and Sirion like a young wild ox.

7 The voice of the Lord splits the flash of lightning;
  the voice of the Lord shakes the wilderness; *
 the Lord shakes the wilderness of Kadesh.

8 **The voice of the Lord makes the oak trees writhe**
  and strips the forests bare; *
 in his temple all cry, 'Glory!'

9 The Lord sits enthroned above the water flood; *
 the Lord sits enthroned as king for evermore.

10 **The Lord shall give strength to his people; ***
 the Lord shall give his people the blessing of peace.

Psalm 29

DIVIDING BEAD

Declare his glory among the nations
and his wonders among all peoples.

Psalm 96.3

Silence is kept.

3RD DECADE *A Song of the New Jerusalem*

1 Arise, shine out, for your light has come, *
 the glory of the Lord is rising upon you.

2 **Though night still covers the earth, ***
 and darkness the peoples;

3 Above you the Holy One arises, *
 and above you God's glory appears.

4 **The nations will come to your light, ***
 and kings to your dawning brightness.

5 Your gates will lie open continually, *
   shut neither by day nor by night.

6 **The sound of violence shall be heard no longer in your land, ***
   or ruin and devastation within your borders.

7 You will call your walls, Salvation, *
   and your gates, Praise.

8 **No more will the sun give you daylight, ***
   nor moonlight shine upon you;

9 But the Lord will be your everlasting light, *
   your God will be your splendour.

10 **For you shall be called the city of God, ***
   the dwelling of the Holy One of Israel.

Isaiah 60.1-3,11a,18,19,14b

DIVIDING BEAD

Give thanks to the Lord, call on his name;
make known his deeds among the nations;
proclaim that his name is exalted.

Isaiah 12.4

Silence is kept.

4TH DECADE *A Song of the Holy City*

1 I saw the holy city *
   coming down out of heaven from God.

2 **I saw a new heaven and a new earth, ***
   for the first heaven and the first earth had passed away
   and the sea was no more.

3 And I saw the holy city, the new Jerusalem, *
  coming down out of heaven from God,
  prepared as a bride adorned for her husband.

4 **And I heard a great voice from the throne saying,***
  'Behold, the dwelling of God is among mortals.

5 'He will dwell with them and they shall be his peoples,*
  and God himself will be with them.

6 **'He will wipe every tear from their eyes,***
  and death shall be no more.

7 'Neither shall there be mourning, nor crying,
    nor pain any more,*
  for the former things have passed away.'

8 **And the One who sat upon the throne said,***
  'Behold, I make all things new.'

9 To the One who sits on the throne and to the Lamb*
  be blessing and honour and glory and might,
    for ever and ever. Amen.

10 **I saw the holy city***
   coming down out of heaven from God.

Revelation 21.1-5a
(vs. 1, 10 CW Refrain)

DIVIDING BEAD

The Spirit of truth, who proceeds from the Father,
he will bear witness to me;
and you also are witnesses.

John 15.26,27

Silence is kept.

5TH DECADE

1 God of our salvation, hope of all the ends of the earth,
   we pray:
   Your kingdom come.

2 That the world may know Jesus Christ as the Prince of Peace,
   we pray:
   Your kingdom come.

3 That all who are estranged and without hope may be brought
   near in the blood of Christ,
   we pray:
   Your kingdom come.

4 That the Church may be one in serving and proclaiming the
   gospel,
   we pray:
   Your kingdom come.

5 That we may be bold to speak the word of God while you
   stretch out your hand to save,
   we pray:
   Your kingdom come.

6 That the Church may be generous in giving, faithful in
   serving, bold in proclaiming,
   we pray:
   Your kingdom come.

7 That the Church may welcome and support all whom God
   calls to faith,
   we pray:
   Your kingdom come.

8 That all who serve the gospel may be kept in safety
    while your word accomplishes its purpose,
    we pray:
Your kingdom come.

9 That all who suffer for the gospel may know the comfort and
    glory of Christ,
    we pray:
Your kingdom come.

10 That the day may come when every knee shall bow
    and every tongue confess that Jesus Christ is Lord,
    we pray:
Your kingdom come.

DIVIDING BEAD

God is light.
In him there is no darkness.

If we live in the light,
as God is in the light,

we have fellowship with one another
and the blood of Jesus, his Son,
purifies us from all sin.

cf 1 John 1.5,7

5TH BEAD

Almighty God,
in Christ you make all things new:
transform the poverty of our nature by the riches of your grace,
and in the renewal of our lives
make known your heavenly glory;
through Jesus Christ our Lord.
Amen.

TRIPLET OF BEADS

4 You are worthy, our Lord and God,
  to receive glory and honour and power.
  For you have created all things,
  and by your will they have their being.

3 You are worthy, O Lamb, for you were slain,
  and by your blood you ransomed for God
  saints from every tribe and language and nation.
  You have made them to be a kingdom and priests
  serving our God, and they will reign with you on earth.
  Revelation 4.11; 5.9b,10

2 To the One who sits on the throne and to the Lamb
  be blessing and honour and glory and might, for ever and ever.
  Amen.

IST BEAD

Heavenly Father,
We offer you our souls and bodies,
our thoughts and words and deeds,
our love for one another.
Unite our wills in your will,
that we may grow
in love and peace
all the days of our life;
through Jesus Christ our Lord.
Amen.

CROSS

May Christ, who sends us to the nations,
give us the power of his Spirit.
Amen.

Let us bless the Lord.
Thanks be to God.

Lent

CROSS

In the name of the Father and of the Son and of the Holy Spirit.
Amen.

The Lord's Prayer

Trusting in the compassion of God,
as our Saviour taught us, so we pray
Our Father in heaven …

(or)

Trusting in the compassion of God,
let us pray with confidence as our Saviour has taught us
Our Father, who art in heaven …

The Apostles' Creed

I believe in God …

1ST BEAD

O God, make speed to save us.
O Lord, make haste to help us.

Hear our voice, O Lord, according to your faithful love,
according to your judgement give us life.

**Glory to the Father and to the Son
and to the Holy Spirit;
as it was in the beginning is now
and shall be for ever. Amen.**

TRIPLET OF BEADS

2 We confess to you our selfishness and lack of love:
   fill us with your Spirit.
   Lord, have mercy.
   Lord, have mercy.

3 We confess to you our fear and failure in sharing our faith:
   fill us with your Spirit.
   Christ, have mercy.
   Christ, have mercy.

4 We confess to you our stubbornness and lack of trust:
   fill us with your Spirit.
   Lord, have mercy.
   Lord, have mercy.

5TH BEAD

Blessed are you, God of compassion and mercy,
to you be praise and glory for ever.
In the darkness of our sin,
your light breaks forth like the dawn
and your healing springs up for deliverance.
As we rejoice in the gift of your saving help,
sustain us with your bountiful Spirit
and open our lips to sing your praise.
Blessed be God, Father, Son and Holy Spirit.
Blessed be God for ever.

DIVIDING BEAD

The Lord is full of compassion and mercy,
slow to anger and of great kindness.

Psalm 103.8

Silence is kept.

Before each decade begins, a prayer intention may be announced.
The cycle of intercession on pages 10–12 may be used.

1ST DECADE   *A Song of Penitence*

1 Have mercy on me, O God, in your great goodness; *
   according to the abundance of your compassion
     blot out my offences.

2 **Wash me thoroughly from my wickedness ***
   and cleanse me from my sin.

3 For I acknowledge my faults *
   and my sin is ever before me.

4 **Against you only have I sinned ***
   and done what is evil in your sight,

5 So that you are justified in your sentence *
   and righteous in your judgement.

6 **Cast me not away from your presence ***
   and take not your holy spirit from me.

7 Give me again the joy of your salvation *
   and sustain me with your gracious spirit;

8 **Then shall I teach your ways to the wicked ***
   and sinners shall return to you.

9 Deliver me from my guilt, O God, the God of my salvation, *
and my tongue shall sing of your righteousness.

Psalm 51.1-5,12-15

10 **Glory to the Father and to the Son and to the Holy Spirit; ***
as it was in the beginning is now and shall be for ever. Amen.

DIVIDING BEAD

For thus said the Lord God, the Holy One of Israel:
In returning and rest you shall be saved;
in quietness and in trust shall be your strength.

Isaiah 30.15

Silence is kept.

2ND DECADE *A Song of the Word of the Lord*

1 Seek the Lord while he may be found, *
call upon him while he is near;

2 **Let the wicked abandon their ways, ***
and the unrighteous their thoughts;

3 Return to the Lord, who will have mercy; *
to our God, who will richly pardon.

4 **'For my thoughts are not your thoughts, ***
neither are your ways my ways,' says the Lord.

5 'For as the heavens are higher than the earth, *
so are my ways higher than your ways
and my thoughts than your thoughts.

6 **'As the rain and the snow come down from above, ***
and return not again but water the earth,

7 'Bringing forth life and giving growth, *
   seed for sowing and bread to eat,

8 **'So is my word that goes forth from my mouth; ***
   it will not return to me fruitless,

9 'But it will accomplish that which I purpose, *
   and succeed in the task I gave it.'

Isaiah 55.6-11

10 **Glory to the Father and to the Son and to the Holy Spirit; ***
   as it was in the beginning is now and shall be for ever. Amen.

DIVIDING BEAD

He was in the wilderness for forty days, tempted by Satan;
and he was with the wild beasts; and the angels waited on him.

Mark 1.13

Silence is kept.

3RD DECADE   *A Song of Humility*

1 Raise us up, O God, *
   that we may live in your presence.

2 **Come, let us return to the Lord ***
   who has torn us and will heal us.

3 God has stricken us *
   and will bind up our wounds.

4 **After two days, he will revive us, ***
   and on the third day will raise us up,
      that we may live in his presence.

5 Let us strive to know the Lord; *
his appearing is as sure as the sunrise.

6 **He will come to us like the showers, ***
like the spring rains that water the earth.

7 'O Ephraim, how shall I deal with you? *
How shall I deal with you, O Judah?

8 **'Your love for me is like the morning mist, ***
like the dew that goes early away.

9 'Therefore, I have hewn them by the prophets, *
and my judgement goes forth as the light.

10 **'For loyalty is my desire and not sacrifice, ***
and the knowledge of God rather than burnt offerings.'

Hosea 6.1-6
(vs. 1 CW Refrain)

DIVIDING BEAD

Be alert at all times, praying that you may have the strength
to escape all these things that will take place,
and to stand before the Son of Man.

Luke 21.36

Silence is kept.

4ᵀᴴ DECADE   *A Song of Manasseh*

1 Lord almighty and God of our ancestors,
you who made heaven and earth in all their glory: *
All things tremble with awe at your presence,
before your great and mighty power.

2 **Immeasurable and unsearchable is your promised mercy, ***
for you are God, Most High.

3 You are full of compassion, long-suffering and very merciful, *
and you relent at human suffering.

4 **O God, according to your great goodness, ***
you have promised forgiveness for repentance
     to those who have sinned against you.

5 The sins I have committed against you *
are more in number than the sands of the sea.

6 **I am not worthy to look up to the height of heaven, ***
because of the multitude of my iniquities.

7 And now I bend the knee of my heart before you,*
imploring your kindness upon me.

8 **I have sinned, O God, I have sinned, ***
and I acknowledge my transgressions.

9 Unworthy as I am, you will save me, *
according to your great mercy.

10 **For all the host of heaven sings your praise, ***
and your glory is for ever and ever.

Manasseh 1a,2,4,6,7a,b,9a,c,11,12,14b,15b

DIVIDING BEAD

The Lord is a great God, O that today you would listen to his voice.
Harden not your hearts.

cf Psalm 95.3,8

Silence is kept.

5TH DECADE

1   From all evil and mischief; from pride, vanity, and hypocrisy;
    from envy, hatred, and malice; and from all evil intent,
    good Lord, deliver us.

2   From sloth, worldliness and love of money;
    from hardness of heart and contempt for your word and
        your laws,
    good Lord, deliver us.

3   From sins of body and mind;
    from the deceits of the world, the flesh and the devil,
    good Lord, deliver us.

4   In all times of sorrow; in all times of joy;
    in the hour of death, and at the day of judgement,
    good Lord, deliver us.

5   By the mystery of your holy incarnation;
    by your birth, childhood and obedience;
    by your baptism, fasting and temptation,
    good Lord, deliver us.

6   By your ministry in word and work;
    by your mighty acts of power;
    and by your preaching of the kingdom,
    good Lord, deliver us.

7   By your agony and trial; by your cross and passion;
    and by your precious death and burial,
    good Lord, deliver us.

8   By your mighty resurrection; by your glorious ascension;
    and by your sending of the Holy Spirit,
    good Lord, deliver us.

9 Give us true repentance;
   forgive us our sins of negligence and ignorance
   and our deliberate sins;
   and grant us the grace of your Holy Spirit
   to amend our lives according to your holy word.
   Holy God,
   holy and strong,
   holy and immortal,
   have mercy upon us.

10 Make our hearts clean, O God;
   and renew a right spirit within us.

from the Litany

DIVIDING BEAD

Jesus, like a mother you gather your people to you;
you are gentle with us as a mother with her children.
Despair turns to hope through your sweet goodness;
through your gentleness we find comfort in fear.
Your warmth gives life to the dead,
your touch makes sinners righteous.
Lord Jesus, in your mercy heal us;
in your love and tenderness remake us.
In your compassion bring grace and forgiveness,
for the beauty of heaven may your love prepare us.

Anselm (1109)

5TH BEAD

Almighty and everlasting God,
you hate nothing that you have made
and forgive the sins of all those who are penitent:
create and make in us new and contrite hearts
that we, worthily lamenting our sins
and acknowledging our wretchedness,

may receive from you, the God of all mercy,
perfect remission and forgiveness;
through Jesus Christ our Lord.
Amen.

TRIPLET OF BEADS

4 The Lord God almighty is our Father:
   he loves us and tenderly cares for us.
3 The Lord Jesus Christ is our Saviour:
   he has redeemed us and will defend us to the end.

2 The Lord, the Holy Spirit, is among us:
   he will lead us in God's holy way.
   To God almighty, Father, Son and Holy Spirit,
   be praise and glory today and for ever. Amen.

1ST BEAD

Jesus said, 'There will be more joy in heaven over one sinner who
repents than over ninety-nine righteous people who need no
repentance.'

Luke 15.7

CROSS

May God bless us, that in us may be found love and humility,
obedience and thanksgiving, discipline, gentleness and peace.
Amen.

Let us bless the Lord.
Thanks be to God.

Passiontide and Holy Week

CROSS

In the name of the Father and of the Son and of the Holy Spirit.
Amen.

The Lord's Prayer

Standing at the foot of the cross,
as our Saviour taught us, so we pray
Our Father in heaven …

(or)

Standing at the foot of the cross,
let us pray with confidence as our Saviour has taught us
Our Father, who art in heaven …

The Apostles' Creed

I believe in God …

1ST BEAD

O God, make speed to save us.
O Lord, make haste to help us.

Let your ways be known upon earth
your saving power among the nations.

**Glory to the Father and to the Son
and to the Holy Spirit;
as it was in the beginning is now
and shall be for ever. Amen.**

TRIPLET OF BEADS

2 O God, you know my foolishness
   and my sins are not hidden from you:
   Lord, have mercy.
   Lord, have mercy.

3 Let not the flood overwhelm me nor the depths swallow me up;
   let not the pit shut its mouth upon me:
   Christ, have mercy.
   Christ, have mercy.

4 Hear me, O Lord, as your loving kindness is good;
   turn to me as your compassion is great:
   Lord, have mercy.
   Lord, have mercy.

5TH BEAD

Blessed are you, Lord God of our salvation,
to you be glory and praise for ever.
As we behold your Son, enthroned on the cross,
stir up in us the fire of your love,
that we may be cleansed from all our sins,
and walk with you in newness of life
singing the praise of him who died
for us and our salvation.
Blessed be God, Father, Son and Holy Spirit.
Blessed be God for ever.

DIVIDING BEAD

I have been crucified with Christ; and it is no longer I who live,
but it is Christ who lives in me.

Galatians 2.19b,20a

Silence is kept.

*Before each decade begins, a prayer intention may be announced.
The cycle of intercession on pages 10–12 may be used.*

1ST DECADE

1 My God, my God, why have you forsaken me, *
   and are so far from my salvation,
      from the words of my distress?

2 **O my God, I cry in the daytime, but you do not answer; ***
   and by night also, but I find no rest.

3 Yet you are the Holy One,
      enthroned upon the praises of Israel. *
   Our forebears trusted in you; they trusted,
      and you delivered them.

4 **They cried out to you and were delivered; ***
   they put their trust in you and were not confounded.

5 But as for me, I am a worm and no man, *
   scorned by all and despised by the people.

6 **All who see me laugh me to scorn; ***
   they curl their lips and wag their heads, saying,

7 'He trusted in the Lord; let him deliver him; *
   let him deliver him, if he delights in him.'

8 **But it is you that took me out of the womb** *
and laid me safe upon my mother's breast.

9 On you was I cast ever since I was born; *
you are my God even from my mother's womb.

10 **Be not far from me, for trouble is near at hand** *
and there is none to help.

Psalm 22.1-11

DIVIDING BEAD

My trust is in you, O Lord.
I have said, 'You are my God.'

Psalm 31.14

Silence is kept.

2ND DECADE

1 Save me, O God, *
for the waters have come up, even to my neck.

2 **I sink in deep mire where there is no foothold;** *
I have come into deep waters and the flood sweeps over me.

3 I have grown weary with crying; my throat is raw; *
my eyes have failed from looking so long for my God.

4 **Those who hate me without any cause** *
are more than the hairs of my head;

5 Those who would destroy me are mighty; *
my enemies accuse me falsely:
    must I now give back what I never stole?

6 **O God, you know my foolishness,** *
and my faults are not hidden from you.

7 Let not those who hope in you
    be put to shame through me, Lord God of hosts; *
  let not those who seek you be disgraced because of me,
    O God of Israel.

8 **For your sake have I suffered reproach;**
    shame has covered my face. *
  I have become a stranger to my kindred,
    an alien to my mother's children.

9 Zeal for your house has eaten me up;
  the scorn of those who scorn you has fallen upon me. *
  I humbled myself with fasting,
  but that was turned to my reproach.

10 **I put on sackcloth also and became a byword among them.***
   Those who sit at the gate murmur against me,
   and the drunkards make songs about me.

Psalm 69.1-13

DIVIDING BEAD

May I never boast of anything except the cross of our Lord Jesus
    Christ,
by which the world has been crucified to me, and I to the world.

Galatians 6.14

Silence is kept.

3RD DECADE   *A Song of Lamentation*

1 Is it nothing to you, all you who pass by? *
  Look and see if there is any sorrow like my sorrow,

2 **Which was brought upon me,** *
  which the Lord inflicted on the day of his fierce anger.
3 For these things I weep; my eyes flow with tears; *
  for a comforter is far from me, one to revive my courage.

4 **Remember my affliction and my bitterness, ***
the wormwood and the gall!

5 But this I call to mind, *
and therefore I have hope:

6 **The steadfast love of the Lord never ceases,**
his mercies never come to an end; *
They are new every morning; great is your faithfulness.

7 'The Lord is my portion,' says my soul,
'therefore I will hope in him.' *
The Lord is good to those who wait for him,
to the soul that seeks him.

8 **It is good that we should wait quietly ***
for the salvation of the Lord.

9 For the Lord will not reject for ever; *
though he causes grief, he will have compassion,

10 **According to the abundance of his steadfast love; ***
for he does not willingly afflict or grieve anyone.

Lamentations 1.12,16a,b; 3.19,21-26,31-33

DIVIDING BEAD

Unless a grain of wheat falls into the earth and dies, it remains just
a single grain;
but if it dies, it bears much fruit.

John 12.24

Silence is kept.

4ᵀᴴ DECADE   *A Song of Jonah*

1 My prayer came to you in your holy temple, *
and you brought up my life from the depths.

2   **I called to you, O God, out of my distress**
        and you answered me; *
    out of the belly of Sheol I cried, and you heard my voice.

3   You cast me into the deep, into the heart of the seas,
        and the flood surrounded me, *
            all your waves and billows passed over me.

4   **Then I said, I am driven away from your sight;** *
    how shall I ever look again upon your holy temple?

5   The waters closed in over me, the deep was round about me; *
        weeds were wrapped around my head
            at the roots of the mountains.

6   **I went down to the land whose bars closed upon me for ever,** *
    yet you brought up my life from the depths, O God.

7   As my life was ebbing away, I remembered you, O God, *
        and my prayer came to you, into your holy temple.

8   **With the voice of thanksgiving, I will sacrifice to you;** *
    what I have vowed I will pay, deliverance belongs to the Lord!

9   Glory to the Father and to the Son and to the Holy Spirit; *
        as it was in the beginning is now and shall be for ever. Amen.

10 **My prayer came to you in your holy temple,** *
    and you brought up my life from the depths.

Jonah 2.2-7,9
(vs. 1, 10: CW Refrain)

DIVIDING BEAD

Blessed are those who are persecuted for righteousness' sake,
for theirs is the kingdom of heaven.

Matthew 5.10

Silence is kept.

115

5ᵀᴴ DECADE

1 Is it nothing to you, all you who pass by?
   Look and see if there is any sorrow like my sorrow
   which was brought upon me,
   which the Lord inflicted on the day of his fierce anger.
   Holy God,
   holy and strong,
   holy and immortal,
   have mercy upon us.

2 O my people, O my Church, what have I done to you,
   or in what have I offended you? Testify against me.
   I led you forth from the land of Egypt,
   and delivered you by the waters of baptism,
   but you have prepared a cross for your Saviour.
   Holy God,
   holy and strong,
   holy and immortal,
   have mercy upon us.

3 I led you through the desert forty years,
     and fed you with manna.
   I brought you through tribulation and penitence,
   and gave you my body, the bread of heaven,
   but you prepared a cross for your Saviour.
   Holy God,
   holy and strong,
   holy and immortal,
   have mercy upon us.

4 What more could I have done for you that I have not done?
   I planted you, my chosen and fairest vineyard,
   I made you the branches of my vine;
   but when I was thirsty, you gave me vinegar to drink,
   and pierced with a spear the side of your Saviour.
   Holy God,
   holy and strong,

holy and immortal,
have mercy upon us.

5 I went before you in a pillar of cloud,
    and you have led me to the judgement hall of Pilate.
    I scourged your enemies and brought you
    to a land of freedom,
    but you have scourged, mocked and beaten me.
    I gave you the water of salvation from the rock,
    but you have given me gall and left me to thirst.
    Holy God,
    holy and strong,
    holy and immortal,
    have mercy upon us.

6 I gave you a royal sceptre,
    and bestowed the keys of the kingdom,
    but you have given me a crown of thorns.
    I raised you on high with great power,
    but you have hanged me on the cross.
    Holy God,
    holy and strong,
    holy and immortal,
    have mercy upon us.

7 My peace I gave, which the world cannot give,
    and washed your feet as a sign of my love,
    but you draw the sword to strike in my name,
    and seek high places in my kingdom.
    I offered you my body and blood,
    but you scatter and deny and abandon me.
    Holy God,
    holy and strong,
    holy and immortal,
    have mercy upon us.

8 I sent the Spirit of truth to guide you,
    and you close your hearts to the Counsellor.

I pray that all may be one in the Father and me,
but you continue to quarrel and divide.
I call you to go and bring forth fruit,
but you cast lots for my clothing.
Holy God,
holy and strong,
holy and immortal,
have mercy upon us.

9 I came to you as the least of your brothers and sisters;
I was hungry and you gave me no food,
I was thirsty and you gave me no drink,
I was a stranger and you did not welcome me,
naked and you did not clothe me,
sick and in prison and you did not visit me.
Holy God,
holy and strong,
holy and immortal,
have mercy upon us.

10 I commanded you to love your neighbour as yourself,
to love and forgive even your enemies;
but you have made vengeance your rule and hate your guide.
Holy God,
holy and strong,
holy and immortal,
have mercy upon us.

from the Good Friday Liturgy

DIVIDING BEAD

Soul of Christ, sanctify me,
body of Christ, save me,
blood of Christ, inebriate me,
water from the side of Christ, wash me.
Passion of Christ, strengthen me.
O good Jesus, hear me:
hide me within your wounds

and never let me be separated from you.
From the wicked enemy defend me,
in the hour of my death, call me
and bid me come to you,
so that with your saints I may praise you
for ever and ever.
Amen.

Anima Christi (14th century)

Silence is kept.

5ᵀᴴ BEAD

(from the Fifth Sunday of Lent)

Most merciful God,
who by the death and resurrection of your Son Jesus Christ
delivered and saved the world:
grant that by faith in him who suffered on the cross
we may triumph in the power of his victory;
through Jesus Christ our Lord.
Amen.

(or, from Palm Sunday)

Almighty and everlasting God,
who in your tender love towards the human race
sent your Son our Saviour Jesus Christ
to take upon him our flesh
and to suffer death upon the cross:
grant that we may follow the example of his patience and humility,
and also be made partakers of his resurrection;
through Jesus Christ our Lord.
Amen.

TRIPLET OF BEADS

4 Here in Christ we gather, love of Christ our calling;
   Christ, our love, is with us, gladness be his greeting;

let us all revere and love him, God eternal.
Loving him, let each love Christ in all his brothers.
God is love, and where true love is, God himself is there.

3 When we Christians gather, members of one Body,
let there be in us no discord, but one spirit;
banished now be anger, strife and every quarrel.
Christ our God be present always here among us.
God is love, and where true love is, God himself is there.

2 Grant us love's fulfilment, joy with all the blessed
when we see your face, O Saviour, in its glory;
shine on us, O purest Light of all creation,
be our bliss while endless ages sing your praises.
God is love, and where true love is, God himself is there.

Ubi caritas
James Quinn SJ

IST BEAD

We adore you, O Christ, and we bless you:
because by your holy cross you have redeemed the world.

CROSS

May Christ, who bore our sins on the cross,
set us free to serve him with joy.
Amen.

Let us bless the Lord.
Thanks be to God.

Easter

CROSS

In the name of the Father and of the Son and of the Holy Spirit.
Amen.

The Lord's Prayer

Rejoicing in God's new creation,
as our Saviour taught us, so we pray
Our Father in heaven …

(or)

Rejoicing in God's new creation,
let us pray with confidence as our Saviour has taught us
Our Father, who art in heaven …

The Apostles' Creed

I believe in God …

1ST BEAD

O God, make speed to save us.
O Lord, make haste to help us.

In your resurrection, O Christ,
let heaven and earth rejoice. Alleluia.

**Glory to the Father and to the Son
and to the Holy Spirit;
as it was in the beginning is now
and shall be for ever. Amen.**

TRIPLET OF BEADS

2 Like Mary at the empty tomb, we fail to grasp the wonder of
   your presence.
   Lord, have mercy.
   Lord, have mercy.

3 Like the disciples behind locked doors, we are afraid to be
   seen as your followers.
   Christ, have mercy.
   Christ, have mercy.

4 Like Thomas in the upper room, we are slow to believe.
   Lord, have mercy.
   Lord, have mercy.

5TH BEAD

Blessed are you, Sovereign Lord,
the God and Father of our Lord Jesus Christ,
to you be glory and praise for ever.
From the deep waters of death
you brought your people to new birth
by raising your Son to life in triumph.
Through him dark death has been destroyed
and radiant life is everywhere restored.
As you call us out of darkness into his marvellous light
may our lives reflect his glory
and our lips repeat the endless song.
Blessed be God, Father, Son and Holy Spirit.
Blessed be God for ever.

DIVIDING BEAD

Sing for joy, O heavens, and exult, O earth;
break forth, O mountains, into singing!
**For the Lord has comforted his people,
and will have compassion on his suffering ones.**

Isaiah 49.13

Silence is kept.

*Before each decade begins, a prayer intention may be announced.
The cycle of intercession on pages 10–12 may be used.*

1ST DECADE

1 Sing to the Lord a new song, *
   for he has done marvellous things.

2 **His own right hand and his holy arm ***
   have won for him the victory.

3 The Lord has made known his salvation; *
   his deliverance has he openly shown in the sight of the nations.

4 **He has remembered his mercy and faithfulness**
      towards the house of Israel, *
   and all the ends of the earth have seen the salvation of
      our God.

5 Sound praises to the Lord, all the earth; *
   break into singing and make music.

6 **Make music to the Lord with the lyre, ***
   with the lyre and the voice of melody.

7 With trumpets and the sound of the horn *
   sound praises before the Lord, the King.

8 **Let the sea thunder and all that fills it,** *
   the world and all that dwell upon it.

9 Let the rivers clap their hands *
   and let the hills ring out together before the Lord,
      for he comes to judge the earth.

10 **In righteousness shall he judge the world** *
    and the peoples with equity.

Psalm 98

DIVIDING BEAD

After his suffering Jesus presented himself alive to them
   by many convincing proofs,
appearing to them over the course of forty days
and speaking about the kingdom of God.

Acts 1.3

Silence is kept.

2ND DECADE   *A Song of Joy with A Song of God's Assembled*

1 O be joyful in the Lord, all the earth; *
   serve the Lord with gladness
      and come before his presence with a song.

2 **Know that the Lord is God;** *
   it is he that has made us and we are his;
      we are his people and the sheep of his pasture.

3 Enter his gates with thanksgiving
      and his courts with praise; *
      give thanks to him and bless his name.

4 **For the Lord is gracious; his steadfast love is everlasting,** *
   and his faithfulness endures from generation to generation.

Psalm 100

5 We have come before God's holy mountain, *
   to the heavenly Jerusalem, the city of the living God.

6 **We have come before countless angels making festival, ***
   before the assembly of the firstborn citizens of heaven.

7 We have come before God, who is judge of all, *
   before the spirits of the just made perfect.

8 **We have come before Jesus, ***
   the mediator of the new covenant.

9 We are receiving a kingdom that cannot be shaken: *
   so let us give thanks and offer to God acceptable worship,

10 **Full of reverence and awe; ***
   for our God is a consuming fire.

Hebrews 12.22-24a,28,29

DIVIDING BEAD

Blessed be the God and Father of our Lord Jesus Christ!
By his great mercy he has given us a new birth into a living hope
through the resurrection of Jesus Christ from the dead.

1 Peter 1.3

Silence is kept.

3ᴿᴰ DECADE   *A Song of Moses and Miriam*

1 In your unfailing love, O Lord, *
   you lead the people whom you have redeemed. Alleluia.

2 **I will sing to the Lord, who has triumphed gloriously, ***
   the horse and his rider he has thrown into the sea.

3 The Lord is my strength and my song *
   and has become my salvation.

4 **This is my God whom I will praise, ***
   the God of my forebears whom I will exalt.

5 The Lord is a warrior, *
   the Lord is his name.

6 **Your right hand, O Lord, is glorious in power: ***
   your right hand, O Lord, shatters the enemy.

7 At the blast of your nostrils, the sea covered them; *
   they sank as lead in the mighty waters.

8 **In your unfailing love, O Lord, ***
   you lead the people whom you have redeemed.

9 And by your invincible strength *
   you will guide them to your holy dwelling.

10 **You will bring them in and plant them, O Lord, ***
   in the sanctuary which your hands have established.

Exodus 15.1b-3,6,10,13,17
(vs. 1 CW Refrain)

DIVIDING BEAD

'The Son of Man is to be betrayed into human hands,
    and they will kill him,
and three days after being killed, he will rise again.'

Mark 9.31

Silence is kept.

4TH DECADE   *The Easter Anthems*

1 The Lord is risen from the tomb *
   who for our sakes hung upon the tree. Alleluia.

2 **Christ our passover has been sacrificed for us:** *
so let us celebrate the feast,

3 not with the old leaven of corruption and wickedness: *
but with the unleavened bread of sincerity and truth.

1 Corinthians 5.7b, 8

4 **Christ once raised from the dead dies no more:** *
death has no more dominion over him.

5 In dying he died to sin once for all: *
in living he lives to God.

6 **See yourselves therefore as dead to sin:** *
and alive to God in Jesus Christ our Lord.

Romans 6.9-11

7 Christ has been raised from the dead: *
the first fruits of those who sleep.

8 **For as by man came death:** *
by man has come also the resurrection of the dead;

9 for as in Adam all die: *
even so in Christ shall all be made alive.

1 Corinthians 15.20-22

10 **Glory to the Father and to the Son and to the Holy Spirit;** *
as it was in the beginning is now and shall be for ever. Amen.

(vs. 1 CW Refrain)

DIVIDING BEAD

Yesterday I was crucified with Christ;
today I am glorified with him.
Yesterday I was dead with Christ;
today I am sharing in his resurrection.
Yesterday I was buried with him;
today I am waking with him from the sleep of death.

Gregory of Nazianzus (389)

Silence is kept.

5ᵀᴴ DECADE   *A Song of Faith*

1 God raised Christ from the dead, *
the Lamb without spot or stain.

2 **Blessed be the God and Father ***
of our Lord Jesus Christ!

3 By his great mercy we have been born anew to a living hope *
through the resurrection of Jesus Christ from the dead,

4 **Into an inheritance that is imperishable, undefiled and**
unfading, *
kept in heaven for you,

5 Who are being protected by the power of God through faith, *
for a salvation ready to be revealed in the last time.

6 **You were ransomed from the futile ways of your ancestors ***
not with perishable things like silver or gold

7 But with the precious blood of Christ *
like that of a lamb without spot or stain.

8 **Through him you have confidence in God,**
who raised him from the dead and gave him glory, *
so that your faith and hope are set on God.

9 Glory to the Father and to the Son and to the Holy Spirit; *
as it was in the beginning is now and shall be for ever. Amen.

10 **God raised Christ from the dead, ***
the Lamb without spot or stain.

1 Peter 1.3-5,18,19,21
(vs. 1, 10 CW Refrain)

DIVIDING BEAD

Blessing and honour and thanksgiving and praise
more than we can utter,
more than we can conceive,
be to you, O most adorable Trinity,
Father, Son, and Holy Spirit,
by all angels, all peoples, all creation,
for ever and ever.

Lancelot Andrewes (1626)

Amen. Alleluia.

Silence is kept.

5ᵀᴴ BEAD

God of life,
who for our redemption gave your only-begotten Son
to the death of the cross,
and by his glorious resurrection
have delivered us from the power of our enemy:
grant us so to die daily to sin,
that we may evermore live with him in the joy of his risen life;
through Jesus Christ our Lord.
Amen.

TRIPLET OF BEADS

4 We give you thanks and praise for the gospel we have received.
Christ died for our sins. Alleluia.
He is risen indeed. Alleluia.

3 Death comes to all through Adam, and sin reigns for a time.
New life without end comes through Christ, and he reigns
for ever. Alleluia.
He is risen indeed. Alleluia.

2 Death, where is your victory? Death, where is your sting?
  Death is swallowed up in victory, the victory you give us
    in Christ. Alleluia.
  He is risen indeed. Alleluia.

1ST BEAD

Jesus said, 'I am the resurrection and the life. Those who
believe in me, even though they die, will live, and everyone
who lives and believes in me will never die.'

John 11.25,26

CROSS

May the risen Christ grant us the joys of eternal life.
Amen.

Let us bless the Lord. Alleluia, alleluia.
Thanks be to God. Alleluia, alleluia.

Pentecost

CROSS

In the name of the Father and of the Son and of the Holy Spirit.
Amen.

The Lord's Prayer

Being made one by the power of the Spirit,
as our Saviour taught us, so we pray
Our Father in heaven …

(or)

Being made one by the power of the Spirit,
let us pray with confidence as our Saviour has taught us
Our Father, who art in heaven …

The Apostles' Creed
I believe in God …

1ST BEAD

O God, make speed to save us.
O Lord, make haste to help us.

Send your Holy Spirit upon us,
and clothe your people with power from on high. Alleluia.

**Glory to the Father and to the Son
and to the Holy Spirit;
as it was in the beginning is now
and shall be for ever. Amen.**

TRIPLET OF BEADS

2 We confess to you our selfishness and lack of love:
   fill us with your Spirit.
   Lord, have mercy.
   Lord, have mercy.

3 We confess to you our fear and failure in sharing our faith:
   fill us with your Spirit.
   Christ, have mercy.
   Christ, have mercy.

4 We confess to you our stubbornness and lack of trust:
   fill us with your Spirit.
   Lord, have mercy.
   Lord, have mercy.

5TH BEAD

Blessed are you, sovereign God, overflowing in love.
With Pentecost dawns the age of the Spirit.
Now the flame of heaven rests on every believer.
Strong and weak, women and men tell out your word;
the young receive visions, the old receive dreams.
With the new wine of the Spirit
they proclaim your reign of love.
Amid the birth pangs of the new creation
the way of light is made known.
Source of freedom, giver of life,
blessed are you, Father, Son and Holy Spirit.
Blessed be God for ever.

DIVIDING BEAD

The Lord is the Spirit, and where the Spirit of the Lord is, there is
     freedom.
And all of us, with unveiled faces, seeing the glory of the
Lord as though reflected in a mirror, are being transformed into
the same image from one degree of glory to another;
for this comes from the Lord, the Spirit.

2 Corinthians 3.17,18

Silence is kept.

*Before each decade begins, a prayer intention may be announced.
The cycle of intercession on pages 10–12 may be used.*

1ˢᵀ DECADE   *A Song of God's Righteousness*

1 Bless the Lord, O my soul, *
   and all that is within me bless his holy name.

2 **Bless the Lord, O my soul, ***
   and forget not all his benefits;

3 Who forgives all your sins *
   and heals all your infirmities;

4 **Who redeems your life from the Pit ***
   and crowns you with faithful love and compassion;

5 Who satisfies you with good things, *
   so that your youth is renewed like an eagle's.

6 **The Lord executes righteousness ***
   and judgement for all who are oppressed.

7 He made his ways known to Moses *
   and his works to the children of Israel.

8 **The Lord has established his throne in heaven,** *
   and his kingdom has dominion over all.

9 Bless the Lord, you angels of his, *
   you mighty ones who do his bidding
      and hearken to the voice of his word.

10 **Bless the Lord, all you his hosts,**
   you ministers of his who do his will. *
   Bless the Lord, all you works of his,
      in all places of his dominion;
   bless the Lord, O my soul.

Psalm 103.1-7,19-22

DIVIDING BEAD

Now there are varieties of gifts, but the same Spirit; and there are
   varieties of services,
but the same Lord; and there are varieties of activities,
but it is the same God who activates all of them in everyone.
To each is given the manifestation of the Spirit for the common
good.

I Corinthians 12.4-7

Silence is kept.

2ND DECADE *A Song of Pilgrimage*

1 While I was still young, *
   I sought Wisdom openly in my prayer.

2 **Before the temple I asked for her,** *
   and I will search for her until the end.

3 From the first blossom to the ripening grape, *
   my heart delighted in her.

4 **My foot walked on the straight path,** *
   from my youth I followed her steps.

134

5 I inclined my ear a little and received her, *
   I found for myself much instruction.

6 **I made progress in Wisdom; ***
   to the One who sent her, I will give glory.

7 I directed my soul to Wisdom, *
   and in purity have I found her.

8 **With her, I gained understanding from the first, ***
   therefore will I never be forsaken.

9 My heart was stirred to seek her, *
   with my tongue will I sing God's praise.

Ecclesiasticus 51.13a,13c-17,20,21a,22b

10 **Glory to the Father and to the Son and to the Holy Spirit;***
    as it was in the beginning is now and shall be for ever. Amen.

DIVIDING BEAD

When you send forth your spirit, they are created,
and you renew the face of the earth.

Psalm 104.32

Silence is kept.

3ᴿᴰ DECADE   *A Song of Tobit*

1 The Spirit of the Father,
   who raised Christ Jesus from the dead, *
   gives life to the people of God. Alleluia.

2 **Blessed be God, who lives for ever, ***
   whose reign endures throughout all ages.

3 Declare God's praise before the nations, *
   you who are the children of Israel.

135

4 **For if our God has scattered you among them,** *
    there too has he shown you his greatness.

5 Exalt him in the sight of the living, *
    because he is our Lord and God and our Father for ever.

6 **Though God punishes you for your wickedness,** *
    mercy will be shown to you all.

7 God will gather you from every nation, *
    from wherever you have been scattered.

8 **When you turn to the Lord with all your heart and soul,** *
    God will hide his face from you no more.

9 See what the Lord has done for you *
    and give thanks with a loud voice.

10 **Praise the Lord of righteousness** *
    and exalt the King of the ages.

Tobit 13.1,3,4-6a
(vs. 1 CW Refrain)

DIVIDING BEAD

God has made us one in Christ.
He has set his seal upon us and, as a pledge of what is to come,
has given the Spirit to dwell in our hearts.
Alleluia.

cf 2 Corinthians 1.22

Silence is kept.

4ᵀᴴ DECADE   *Song of Ezekiel with A Song of God's Children*

1 I will take you from the nations, *
    and gather you from all the countries.

2 **I will sprinkle clean water upon you,** *
  and you shall be clean from all your uncleannesses.

3 A new heart I will give you, and put a new spirit within you, *
  and I will remove from your body the heart of stone
  and give you a heart of flesh.

4 **You shall be my people,** *
  and I will be your God.

Ezekiel 36.24-26,28b

5 The law of the Spirit of life in Christ Jesus *
  has set us free from the law of sin and death.

6 **All who are led by the Spirit of God are children of God;** *
  for we have received the Spirit that enables us to cry,
    'Abba, Father'.

7 The Spirit himself bears witness that we are children of God *
  and if God's children, then heirs of God;

8 **If heirs of God, then fellow-heirs with Christ;** *
  since we suffer with him now, that we may be glorified
    with him.

9 These sufferings that we now endure *
  are not worth comparing to the glory that shall be revealed.

10 **For the creation waits with eager longing** *
  for the revealing of the children of God.

Romans 8.2,14,15b-19

DIVIDING BEAD

'Go therefore and make disciples of all nations,
baptizing them in the name of the Father and of the Son and of
  the Holy Spirit,

and teaching them to obey everything that I have commanded
you.
And remember,
I am with you always, to the end of the age.'

Matthew 28.19,20

Silence is kept.

5ᵀᴴ DECADE   *Veni Sancte Spiritus – Come, Holy Spirit*

1 Come Holy Spirit; *
   Send down from heaven's height your radiant light.

2 **Come, lamp of every heart, ***
   come, parent of the poor; all gifts are yours.

3 Comforter beyond all comforting, *
   sweet unexpected guest, sweetly refresh.

4 **Rest in hard labour, ***
   coolness in heavy heat, hurt soul's relief.

5 Refill the secret hearts of your faithful, *
   O most blessed light.

6 **Without your holy power nothing can bear your light, ***
   nothing is free from sin.

7 Wash all that is filthy, water all that is parched, *
   heal what is hurt within.

8 **Bend all that is rigid, warm all that has frozen hard, ***
   lead back the lost.

9 Give to your faithful ones, who come in simple trust, *
   your sevenfold mystery.

10 **Give virtue its reward,** *
     give, in the end, salvation and joy that has no end.

after the Golden Sequence

DIVIDING BEAD

I am giving you worship with all my life,
I am giving you obedience with all my power,
I am giving you praise with all my strength,
I am giving you honour with all my speech.

I am giving you love with all my heart,
I am giving you affection with all my sense,
I am giving you my being with all my mind,
I am giving you my soul, O most high and holy God.

Praise to the Father,
Praise to the Son,
Praise to the Spirit,
The Three in One.

adapted from Alexander Carmichael,
Carmina Gadelica (1900)

Silence is kept.

5TH BEAD

Holy Spirit, sent by the Father,
ignite in us your holy fire;
strengthen your children with the gift of faith,
revive your Church with the breath of love,
and renew the face of the earth,
through Jesus Christ our Lord.
Amen.

TRIPLET OF BEADS

4 Be with us, Spirit of God;
nothing can separate us from your love.

3 Breathe on us, breath of God;
fill us with your saving power.

2 Speak in us, wisdom of God;
bring strength, healing, and peace.

1ST BEAD

Jesus said, 'Peace be with you. As the Father has sent me,
so I send you.' When he had said this, he breathed on them and
said to them,
'Receive the Holy Spirit.'

John 20.21,22

CROSS

May the Spirit kindle in us the fire of God's love.
Amen.

Let us bless the Lord.
Thanks be to God.

All Saints to Advent

CROSS

In the name of the Father and of the Son and of the Holy Spirit.
Amen.

The Lord's Prayer

Uniting our prayers with the whole company of heaven,
as our Saviour taught us, so we pray
Our Father in heaven …

(or)

Uniting our prayers with the whole company of heaven,
let us pray with confidence as our Saviour has taught us
Our Father, who art in heaven …

The Apostles' Creed

I believe in God …

1ST BEAD

O God, make speed to save us.
O Lord, make haste to help us.

Your faithful servants bless you.
They make known the glory of your kingdom.

**Glory to the Father and to the Son
and to the Holy Spirit;
as it was in the beginning is now
and shall be for ever. Amen.**

TRIPLET OF BEADS

2 Lord, you are gracious and compassionate:
Lord, have mercy.
Lord, have mercy.

3 You are loving to all
and your mercy is over all your creation:
Christ, have mercy.
Christ, have mercy.

4 Your faithful servants bless your name
and speak of the glory of your kingdom:
Lord, have mercy.
Lord, have mercy.

5TH BEAD

Blessed are you, Sovereign God,
ruler and judge of all,
to you be praise and glory for ever.
In the darkness of this age that is passing away
may the light of your presence which the saints enjoy
surround our steps as we journey on.
May we reflect your glory this day
and so be made ready to see your face
in the heavenly city where night shall be no more.
Blessed be God, Father, Son and Holy Spirit.
Blessed be God for ever.

DIVIDING BEAD

Blessed is the King who comes in the name of the Lord.
Peace in heaven and glory in the highest heaven.

Luke 19.38

Silence is kept.

142

Before each decade begins, a prayer intention may be announced.
The cycle of intercession on pages 10–12 may be used.

1ST DECADE

1 As the deer longs for the water brooks, *
   so longs my soul for you, O God.

2 **My soul is athirst for God, even for the living God; ***
   when shall I come before the presence of God?

3 My tears have been my bread day and night, *
   while all day long they say to me, 'Where is now your God?'

4 **Now when I think on these things, I pour out my soul: ***
   how I went with the multitude
     and led the procession to the house of God,

5 With the voice of praise and thanksgiving, *
   among those who kept holy day.

6 **Why are you so full of heaviness, O my soul, ***
   and why are you so disquieted within me?

7 O put your trust in God; *
   for I will yet give him thanks,
     who is the help of my countenance, and my God.

8 **The Lord will grant his loving-kindness in the daytime; ***
   through the night his song will be with me,
     a prayer to the God of my life.

9 Why are you so full of heaviness, O my soul, *
   and why are you so disquieted within me?

10 **O put your trust in God; ***
   for I will yet give him thanks,
     who is the help of my countenance, and my God.

Psalm 42.1-7,10,13,14

DIVIDING BEAD

Jesus Christ is the firstborn from the dead;
to him be glory and power for ever and ever.

cf Colossians 1.18

Silence is kept.

2ND DECADE   *A Song of Baruch*

1 Lead us, O God, with joy *
   to walk in the light of glory.

2 **Arise, O Jerusalem, stand upon the height: ***
   look to the east and see your children,

3 Gathered from the west and the east *
   at the word of the Holy One.

4 **They rejoice that God has remembered them ***
   and has brought them back to you.

5 For God has ordered that every high mountain *
   and the everlasting hills be made low,

6 **And the valleys filled up to make level ground ***
   so that they may walk safely in the glory of God.

7 The woods and every fragrant tree *
   have shaded them at God's command.

8 **For God will lead his people with joy in the light of his glory ***
   with the mercy and righteousness that comes from God.

Baruch 5.5,6c,7-9

9 Glory to the Father and to the Son and to the Holy Spirit; *
   as it was in the beginning is now and shall be for ever. Amen.

10 **Lead us, O God, with joy** *
to walk in the light of glory.

(vs. 1,10 CW Refrain)

DIVIDING BEAD

Blessed are the poor in spirit,
for theirs is the kingdom of heaven.

Matthew 5.3

Silence is kept.

3ᴿᴰ DECADE *A Song of the Redeemed*

1 Behold, a great multitude*
which no one could number,

2 **From every nation, from all tribes and peoples and tongues,** *
standing before the throne and the Lamb.

3 They were clothed in white robes
and had palms in their hands, *
and they cried with a loud voice, saying,

4 **'Salvation belongs to our God who sits on the throne,** *
and to the Lamb.'

5 These are they who have come out of the great tribulation, *
they have washed their robes
and made them white in the blood of the Lamb;

6 **Therefore they stand before the throne of God,** *
whom they serve day and night within the temple.

7 And the One who sits upon the throne *
will shelter them with his presence.

8 **They shall never again feel hunger or thirst,** *
the sun shall not strike them, nor any scorching heat.

9 For the Lamb at the heart of the throne will be their
   Shepherd, *
   He will guide them to springs of living water,
   and God will wipe away every tear from their eyes.

10 **To the One who sits on the throne and to the Lamb ***
   be blessing and honour and glory and might,
   for ever and ever. Amen.

Revelation 7.9, 10, 14b-17

DIVIDING BEAD

To crown all things there must be love,
to bind all together and complete the whole.
Let the peace of Christ rule in our hearts.

Colossians 3.14,15

Silence is kept.

4TH DECADE   *A Song of Francis of Assisi*

1 Most High, all powerful, good Lord,
  to you be praise, glory, honour and all blessing *
  Only to you, Most High, do they belong
  and no one is worthy to call upon your name.

2 **May you be praised, my Lord, with all your creatures,**
  especially brother sun,
  through whom you lighten the day for us.*
  He is beautiful and radiant with great splendour;
  he signifies you, O Most High.

3 Be praised, my Lord, for sister moon and the stars: *
  clear and precious and lovely, they are formed in heaven.

4 **Be praised, my Lord, for brother wind;***
  for air and clouds, clear skies and all weathers,
  by which you give sustenance to your creatures.

146

5 Be praised, my Lord, for sister water,
   who is very useful and humble and precious and pure.*
   Be praised, my Lord, for brother fire,
       by whom the night is illumined for us:
   he is beautiful and cheerful, full of power and strength.

6 **Be praised, my Lord, for our sister, mother earth,**
   who sustains and governs us*
   and produces diverse fruits and coloured flowers and grass.

7 Be praised, my Lord, by all those who forgive for love of you
   and who bear weakness and tribulation.*
   Blessed are those who bear them in peace:
   for you, Most High, they will be crowned.

8 **Be praised, my Lord, for our sister, the death of the body,**
   from which no one living is able to flee;*
       woe to those who are dying in mortal sin.

9 Blessed are those who are found doing your most holy will,*
   for the second death will do them no harm.

10 **Praise and bless my Lord and give him thanks***
    and serve him with great humility.

Francis of Assisi

DIVIDING BEAD

We give you thanks
that he is the King of glory,
who overcomes the sting of death
and opens the kingdom of heaven to all believers.
He is seated at your right hand in glory
and we believe that he will come to be our judge.

Silence is kept.

5TH DECADE

1 For the gift of his Spirit:
blessed be Christ.

2 For the catholic Church:
blessed be Christ.

3 For the means of grace:
blessed be Christ.

4 For the hope of glory:
blessed be Christ.

5 For the triumphs of his gospel:
blessed be Christ.

6 For the lives of his saints:
blessed be Christ.

7 In joy and in sorrow:
blessed be Christ.

8 In life and in death:
blessed be Christ.

9 Now and to the end of the ages:
blessed be Christ.

from A Litany of the Resurrection

10 Glory to the Father and to the Son and to the Holy Spirit;
as it was in the beginning is now and shall be for ever. Amen.

DIVIDING BEAD

Great and wonderful are your deeds,
Lord God the Almighty.

Just and true are your ways,
O ruler of the nations.
Who shall not revere and praise your name, O Lord?
for you alone are holy.
All nations shall come and worship in your presence:
for your just dealings have been revealed.

Revelation 15.3,4

Silence is kept.

5ᵀᴴ BEAD

Almighty God,
you have knit together your elect
in one communion and fellowship
in the mystical body of your Son Christ our Lord:
give us grace so to follow your blessed saints
in all virtuous and godly living
that we may come to those inexpressible joys
that you have prepared for those who truly love you;
through Jesus Christ our Lord.
Amen.

TRIPLET OF BEADS

4 Glory to God in the highest, and peace to his people on earth.
   Lord God, heavenly King, almighty God and Father,
   we worship you, we give you thanks,
   we praise you for your glory.

3 Lord Jesus Christ, only Son of the Father, Lord God,
      Lamb of God,
   you take away the sin of the world:
   have mercy on us;
   you are seated at the right hand of the Father:
   receive our prayer.

2 For you alone are the Holy One, you alone are the Lord,
   you alone are the Most High, Jesus Christ,
   with the Holy Spirit, in the glory of God the Father. Amen.

Gloria in Excelsis – A Song of God's Glory

IST BEAD

Come, my Light, and illumine my darkness.
Come, my Life, and revive me from death.
Come, my Physician, and heal my wounds.
Come, Flame of divine love, and burn up the thorns of my sins,
kindling my heart with the flame of your love.
Come, my King, sit upon the throne of my heart and reign there,
for you alone are my King and my Lord.
Amen.

Dimitri of Rostov (1709)

CROSS

May Christ, who has opened the kingdom of heaven,
bring us to reign with him in glory.
Amen.

Let us bless the Lord.
Thanks be to God.

Index of Biblical and Other Readings

FOR THE TRIPLET OF BEADS AND THE DECADES

Isaiah 11.1,2,3b-4a,6,9 [Christmas] 83
Isaiah 12.2-6 [Monday] 56
Isaiah 26.1-4,7-9,12 [Tuesday] 57
Isaiah 35.1,2b-4a,4c-6,10 [Advent] 72
from Isaiah 43 [Thursday] 60
cf Isaiah 55 [Morning] 16
Isaiah 55.6-11 [Lent] 102
Isaiah 60.1-3,11a,18,19,14b [Epiphany] 93
Isaiah 61.1-3,11,6a [Evening Prayer] 37
Isaiah 61.10-11; 62: 1-3 [Through the Day] 27
Lamentations 1.12,16a,b; 3.19,21-26,31-33 [Passiontide] 113
Ezekiel 36.24-26,28b [Pentecost] 136
Hosea 6.1-6 [Lent] 103
Jonah 2.2-7,9 [Passiontide] 114

Tobit 13.1,3,4-6a [Pentecost] 135
Ecclesiasticus 51.13a, 13c-17, 20, 21a, 22b [Pentecost] 134
Baruch 5.5,6c,7-9 [All Saints] 144
The Song of the Three 35-37, 60-65 [Through the Day] 28
The Song of the Three 35-65 [Sunday] 54
Manasseh 1a, 2, 4, 6, 7a, b, 9a, c, 11, 12, 14b, 15b [Lent] 104

Matthew 5.3-10 [Night] 48
Luke 1.46-55 [Evening] 40
Luke 1.68-79 [Morning, Advent] 20, 76
Luke 2.29-32 [Night] 51
from John 1 [Christmas] 88

Romans 4.24,25; 5.1-5,8,9,11 [Evening] 38
Romans 8.2,14,15b-19 [Pentecost] 137
1 Corinthians 13.4-13 [Through the Day] 29
Ephesians 1.3-10 [Christmas] 85
Philippians 2.5-11 [Christmas] 88
from Colossians 3 [Morning] 23
Colossians 1.13-18a,19,20a [Morning] 19
Hebrews 12.22-24a,28,29 [Easter] 125
1 Peter 1.3-5,18,19,21 [Easter] 128
1 John 1.1, 5-9 [Night] 47
from 1 John 1 [Christmas] 80
1 John 4.7-11,12b [Evening] 42
Revelation 4.11; 5.9b,10 [Epiphany] 97
Revelation 7.9, 10, 14b-17 [All Saints] 145
Revelation 21.1-5a [Epiphany] 94
Revelation 21.22-26; 22.1,2b,d,3b,4 [Evening, Easter] 39
Revelation 22.12-14,16,17 [Advent] 73

FOR THE DIVIDING BEADS